■ ■ ■ ■ ■ ■ ■ ■ ORANGE

Concepts in SCIENCE

■■■■■■■ ORANGE

Concepts in SCIENCE

SECOND EDITION

PAUL F. BRANDWEIN

ELIZABETH K. COOPER

PAUL E. BLACKWOOD

ELIZABETH B. HONE

HARCOURT, BRACE & WORLD, INC.

New York   Chicago   San Francisco   Atlanta   Dallas

EDITORIAL CONSULTANTS

Hubert N. Alyea	George M. Crawford	Hy Ruchlis
Esther L. Bossung	Herbert Drapkin	Marguerite Smith
Herman R. Branson	Thomas P. Fraser	Robert Stollberg
Matthew Brennan	Ruth McDonald	Violet Strahler
Annie Sue Brown	Clifford R. Nelson	Richard M. Sutton
R. Will Burnett	Helio C. Parreira	Fletcher G. Watson

PICTURE CREDITS

Cover: C. Douglas from Photo Library, Inc. **Unit One:** pp. 2, 4, 5, 9, 12, 13, Harbrace; p. 19, Harbrace; p. 20, Gene Ahrens from Shostal; p. 24, Armstrong Cork Company. **Unit Two:** p. 28, Ray Hunold; pp. 30, 31, 33, Harbrace; p. 38, Solar Energy Society; pp. 39, 41, 42, 45, 47, 49, 58, 59, Harbrace. **Unit Three:** p. 60, Dr. E. R. Degginger; pp. 62, 63, 66, 67, 72, Harbrace; p. 73, Jerry Cooke from Photo Researchers; p. 77, Harbrace; p. 80, Louis Renault from Photo Researchers; pp. 81, 82, Harbrace; p. 83, Steve McCutcheon; p. 87, Harbrace; p. 88, George Holton from Photo Researchers; p. 89, Harbrace; p. 90, Infilco; p. 91, George Leavens from Photo Researchers. **Unit Four:** p. 98, Harbrace; pp. 100, 101, 103, 104, 105, 107, 108, 109, 110, 111, 112, 113, 115, 116, 117, 119, 120, 121, 124, 125, 131, Harbrace. **Unit Five:** p. 134, J. P. Jackson; p. 136, Harbrace; p. 138, Kansas State University; p. 139: left, Ray Manley from Shostal; right, Doug Fulton from Photo Researchers; p. 142: left, Kansas State University; right, Grant Heilman; p. 143, Harbrace; p. 144, Allied Chemical Corporation; pp. 146, 147, 148, 149, 150, 153, Harbrace; p. 159: top, middle, Harbrace; bottom, Walter Dawn; p. 160: top left, courtesy CCM: General Biological, Inc., Chicago; bottom left, John Vandell from Shostal; bottom right, Stephen Collins from Photo Researchers; p. 161, Harbrace; p. 162, Walter Dawn; p. 163, Al Lowry from Photo Researchers; p. 166, Russ Kinne from Photo Researchers; p. 167, Ansel Adams from Magnum; p. 169, Charles R. Belinky from Photo Researchers. **Unit Six:** p. 174, U.S. Bureau of Sport Fisheries and Wildlife; p. 177, Harbrace; p. 181, Bob and Ira Spring; p. 183: top, Holden Hayden from Shostal; bottom, Bob and Ira Spring; p. 187, Harbrace; p. 190, Harbrace; p. 193, Bob and Ira Spring; p. 198, Harbrace; p. 199, Grant Heilman; p. 203, Harbrace; p. 204, Olaf Sööt from Photo Researchers; p. 209, Jim Theologos; pp. 212, 213, Dr. E. R. Degginger; p. 214, Harbrace. **Unit Seven:** p. 218, J. H. Burnett from Shostal; pp. 220, 221, Harbrace; p. 222, Carl Frank from Photo Researchers; p. 223, Russ Kinne from Photo Researchers; p. 224, National Park Service; p. 225, Harbrace; pp. 226, 227, Russ Kinne from Photo Researchers; p. 228, Eugene A. Visconti, Pennsylvania Turnpike Commission; p. 229, Harbrace; p. 230, Russ Kinne from Photo Researchers; pp. 231, 232, 233, 234, 235, Harbrace; p. 236, Robert Toby from Freelance Photographers Guild; p. 238, Corps of Army Engineers, U.S. Army; p. 239, Sky Hixson from Shostal; pp. 241, 242, Harbrace; p. 243, Steve McCutcheon; p. 246, Camera Hawaii from FPG; p. 253, Franklin Photo Agency, Norwood, Mass. **Unit Eight:** p. 256, Mount Wilson and Palomar Observatories; p. 257, Harbrace; p. 259, Wide World; p. 261: top, tapestry of Queen Mathilde, Museum, Bayeux, France; bottom, Bettmann Archives; p. 267, Harbrace; p. 271, Yerkes Observatory; p. 273: top, Josef Muench; bottom, Harbrace; p. 275, Harbrace; p. 276, A Lick Observatory Photograph; p. 280, Jerry Cooke from Photo Researchers; p. 281, William C. Darrah, *Principles of Paleobotany*, 2nd edition, copyright © 1960, The Ronald Press Company; drawn by G. W. Dillon; p. 282, Mount Wilson and Palomar Observatories; p. 283, United Press International. **Probing with a Microscope:** pp. 284, 285, 286, 287, 288, 289, 290, 291, 292, Harbrace; p. 293: bottom left, Harbrace; all others, Walter Dawn; p. 295: top, Harbrace; bottom, Eric V. Grave; p. 297, Harbrace; pp. 298, 299, Walter Dawn.

ILLUSTRATORS

All artwork done by Diamond Art Studio, with the exception of p. 1,
Chuck Liese for Dick Morrill Studio.

ISBN 0-15-366250-6

CONTENTS

About This Book

Imagine that you are pouring milk. You get a cup ready. You hold the pitcher right over the cup. You begin to pour the milk—very, very carefully. But you cannot get any milk into the cup. Instead of flowing down, the milk starts to rise. It rises higher and higher. Finally it rises so high that it is out of sight!

Of course you would be astonished. Anyone would be. We expect milk and water to flow downward, just as we expect stones and other objects to fall down. They always have. These are regular events, aren't they? Things always fall downward, just as summer always follows spring.

We depend on regular events, don't we? It would be a strange world if you could not tell what was going to happen when you started to pour milk into a cup or pushed a door to open it. It would be so strange a world, if regular events stopped being regular, that we could not live in it.

This book is about regular events. It is about events that can be predicted because scientists have found out what makes them regular.

UNIT ONE

THE BOUNCE
OF SOUND

Think for a moment about how many different sounds you hear around you every day.

The tick of a clock. The roar of a jet plane. The bark of a dog. A friend's voice. Wind in the trees. The rumble of thunder. The twang of a guitar. A door closing. The squeak of chalk on the board. The thud of a bass drum. The rustle of paper. A sneeze. A cat's purr. The patter of rain. Bells and buzzers. Auto horns. What other kinds of sounds would you add to the list?

The boy hears sounds coming from the shell. How do you explain these sounds? After Unit One, try to answer this question again. Perhaps you can then improve your answer.

No matter what sounds you listen to, no matter how different they seem, they are all alike in certain ways.

How are all sounds alike? Let's investigate.

1. Making a Sound

What is sound? How is sound made? Let's look for some answers to these questions. Let's look for answers as scientists do. This is a book about how scientists look for answers to questions, and what scientists find out.

There are different ways of answering a question, you know. If you ask an artist "What is sound?" he might paint you a picture for an answer. If you ask a composer what sound is, he might compose a piece of music for his answer. If you ask a doctor what sound is, he might tell you what sound does to your ear. If you ask a scientist what sound is, what will he say? We are going to look at the answer that scientists give. We are also going to see how scientists look for answers, for scientists have special ways of investigation.

As you go on in science, you will get to know more and more about how scientists investigate. How? By investigating! Like them, you will observe carefully. You will ask: What do my observations mean? You will, of course, reason about what you see and try to explain it. You will search into what others have learned before you.

Each blue page of this book has two kinds of investigations: **An Investigation** and an **Additional Investigation.** By doing such investigations, you discover how to investigate on your own.

How is sound made? See for yourself. Begin with the investigations opposite. INVESTIGATE

Sound and Movement

The rubber band makes a sound. The ruler makes a sound. When they make a sound, they *move*.

Putting a finger on the moving rubber band stops the movement. The sound stops too. Stopping the moving ruler stops the sound there, too.

It seems that to make a sound, the rubber band and the ruler must *move*.

This is true for more than rubber bands and rulers. Touch a bell when it is ringing. You will feel the metal moving. ■ See the picture marked with a blue square.

AN INVESTIGATION into the Making of a Sound

Needed: a ruler, a rubber band, a pie tin or saucer

Stretch the rubber band around the pie tin or saucer. Pluck the rubber band with a finger so that it makes a sound. ■ See the picture marked with a square. What does the rubber band do while you hear the sound? ●

What happens to the rubber band as the sound dies away and stops?

Pluck the rubber band. Before the sound dies away, put your finger on the band. What happens to the band? What happens to the sound?

Hold down one end of the ruler firmly on a table. Pluck the free end of the ruler. ▲ What does the ruler do while the sound is heard?

Pluck the free end of the ruler again. Before the sound stops, stop the ruler with your hand. What happens to the sound?

Look closely at the ruler or rubber band when it is making a sound. (The ruler moves slowly if you make the free end long.) How does each move?

Additional Investigation: Can you make a sound with the ruler or the rubber band without its moving?

■

●

▲

Put your finger lightly on a sounding piano string. You will feel it moving. Touch the string of a double bass or a guitar while it is sounding. You will feel it moving. Touch a drumhead just after the drummer has hit it. It is moving.

The trumpet player's lips move when he blows air into his trumpet. Inside your throat there is something that moves when you make a sound. Put your hand on your throat, sing "ah," and feel the movement.

Wherever there is a sound, something is moving to make that sound. Many investigations and experiments, by many scientists, have shown it is so.

Think again of all the different sounds you can hear. Yet no matter how different the sounds are, they are all alike in this.

To make sound, something moves.

To and Fro

To make sound, there must be movement. What kind of motion must it be?

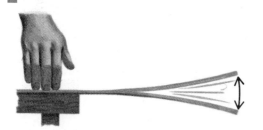

Could you see how the ruler moved as it made a sound? It moved up and down. It swung one way and then the other way, to and fro. ■

Could you observe how the rubber band moved as it made a sound? It swung back and forth, to and fro. ● If you wish, you can see this movement in slow motion. Make a chain of rubber bands about 2 feet long. Fasten one end to a doorknob or table leg. Stretch the chain just a little and pluck it. It will move to and fro, slowly enough for you to see.

It is this to-and-fro movement that makes sound. Scientists have a name for this kind of movement. It is called **vibration** (vy·BRAY·sh'n). The rubber band vibrates as it moves to and fro and makes a sound. The ruler vibrates as it makes a sound. A piano string and a guitar string vibrate as they make sounds. The trumpet player's lips vibrate. The bass drum vibrates. Inside your throat something must vibrate in order for you to speak or sing.

●

Whenever you hear a sound, something is vibrating. Something is moving back and forth.

Does this mean that whenever something is vibrating, you hear a sound? Try it and see. Vibrate your hand, like a fan. Vibrate the chain of rubber bands in slow motion. No sound is heard. Things can vibrate without making a sound.

Whenever you hear a sound, however, something is vibrating.

BEFORE YOU GO ON Study these statements and choose the correct responses. Your study will help fix in your mind the main concept of this section.

1. Whenever there is a sound, something is
   a. moving   b. being plucked

2. When a thing vibrates, it moves
   a. very quickly   b. to and fro

3. As you sing, something in your throat
   a. vibrates   b. stops vibrating

USING WHAT YOU KNOW When a ball hits a tennis racket, there is a sound. What might be vibrating?

ON YOUR OWN Get a thick rubber band and a thin rubber band of about the same length. Hook one end of each rubber band over a doorknob. Stretch both bands the same distance. Pluck each band. What do you observe?

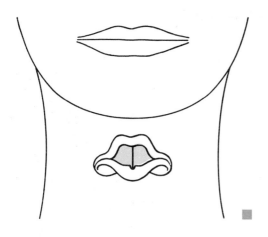

2. High and Low

Put your hand on your throat and hum a note. You can feel something vibrating in your throat and making the sound. Your vocal cords are vibrating, right inside your throat. ■
When you speak or sing or hum, your vocal cords vibrate to make the sound.

Hum as high a note as you can. Hum as low a note as you can. We say that the high note has a high **pitch.** The low note has a low pitch. When you change from one note to another, the pitch changes.

You can feel muscles in your throat moving as you change pitch. What are your vocal cords doing that makes the pitch of the sound change? Find out with the help of a comb and a cardboard. Try the investigation on the opposite page. `INVESTIGATE`

Fast and Slow

What happens as you draw a piece of cardboard very slowly along the teeth of a comb? The cardboard catches on a tooth and is pulled back a little. Then the cardboard slips off the tooth and springs forward. The next tooth pulls the cardboard back again. Back and forth goes the edge of the cardboard along the comb. ●

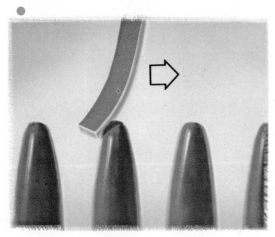

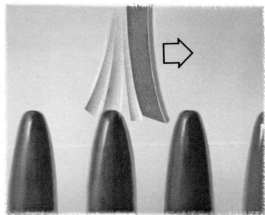

AN INVESTIGATION into High and Low Pitch

Needed: a comb, a piece of thin, stiff cardboard

Hold the comb in one hand and the cardboard in the other, like this.■ Hold the cardboard lightly but firmly.

Pull the cardboard slowly and steadily along the teeth of the comb.● Listen to the pitch of the sound that is made.

Now pull the cardboard faster along the teeth. Does the pitch change? Does it get higher, or does it get lower? Listen carefully.

Move the cardboard along the teeth of the comb at different speeds until you are sure what happens to the pitch.

Now draw the cardboard along the teeth very slowly. Observe what happens to the cardboard. How do the teeth make the cardboard vibrate?

Moving the cardboard quickly along the comb makes fast vibrations. Moving the cardboard slowly makes slow vibrations.

What happens to the pitch when the vibrations are slow? What happens to the pitch when the vibrations are fast?

Additional Investigation: Next time you are in a bus, listen to the sound of the motor. What happens to the pitch as the bus moves faster? Why?

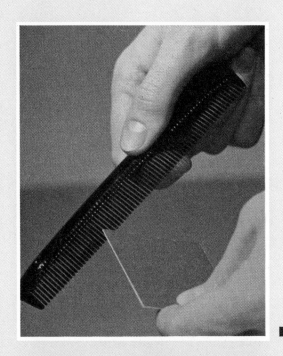

■

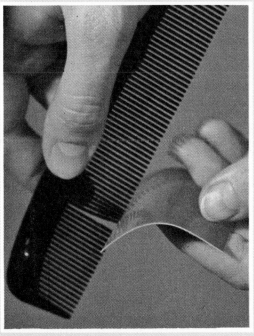

●

9

on a piano comes from a string that is made to vibrate slowly.

The buzz of a mosquito has a higher pitch than the hum of a bee. Their vibrating wings make the sound. ■ Which one's wings are vibrating faster?

Changing the Pitch

Take a piece of thick, heavy string about 2 feet long. Tie one end to something firm, such as a doorknob. Pull the other end hard and pluck the string. Is the pitch of the sound low or high? Take another piece of string about 2 feet long, but thin and light. Stretch it tight. But before you pluck it, make a guess. Will its pitch be higher or lower than the heavy string?

The thinner string can vibrate more quickly than the thicker one. Its pitch will be higher. The thicker string, being heavier, moves more slowly. Its vibrations are slower. Its pitch is lower. You may have noticed that the strings that make the low notes on a piano or a guitar or a double bass are thicker and heavier than the other strings.

Perhaps you have already found out that tightening or loosening a rubber band stretched around a pie tin or saucer made its pitch change.

The cardboard is vibrating. You can make it vibrate slowly or quickly by moving it slowly or quickly along the comb.

What happens to the pitch of the sound the cardboard makes? It isn't a very clear pitch, certainly, but it does change. As the vibrations get faster, the pitch goes higher. As the vibrations get slower, the pitch goes lower.

The higher the pitch of the sound, the faster the vibrations that make the sound. The lower the pitch, the slower the vibrations. This holds good for *all* sounds, not just for combs and cardboard. When you hum a high note, your vocal cords are vibrating faster than when you hum a low note. The squeak of chalk on the chalkboard has a very high pitch, made by very fast vibrations. The lowest note

This is another way of making vibrations go faster or slower. Tightening a string makes it vibrate faster, and loosening it makes it vibrate slower. You may have seen a violinist tighten or loosen a string.

There are still other ways of changing the pitch of a sound. You can be sure of one thing about all of the ways, however. In order to change the pitch, the speed of the vibrations must change.

BEFORE YOU GO ON Study these statements and choose the correct responses. Your study will help fix in your mind the main concept of this section.

1. A policeman's whistle makes a high sound. We say the whistle has a
    a. high pitch   b. low pitch

2. As the pitch of a sound goes lower, the vibrations go
    a. faster   b. more slowly

3. The thickest and heaviest string on a guitar plays
    a. the highest pitch   b. the lowest pitch

USING WHAT YOU KNOW A bass viol can make a sound of very low pitch. A violin can make a very high-pitched sound. Why?

ON YOUR OWN Make a stringed instrument using rubber bands. Make your instrument with rubber bands placed in such a way that you will get low-pitched and high-pitched sounds.

3. Pushing and Pulling Molecules

You see a friend on the other side of the street. Your friend does not see you. "Hi," you call. Your friend turns around.

What makes your friend turn around?

When you call "Hi," your vocal cords vibrate. Their vibration makes sound. But your friend is some distance away. How does he know that your vocal cords are vibrating, when you are on the other side of the street? How do the vibrations get from you to him?

Try the investigation on the opposite page. It will give you a clue to the explanation. INVESTIGATE

Waves

A **wave** can be sent along a rope by flipping the end of the rope. Flip the end of the rope quickly three or four times, and three or four waves will run along the rope, one after the other. Isn't this flipping movement a vibration? You can send waves along a rope by vibrating the end of it.

Dip a finger in calm water. Move the finger back and forth. You can send waves in water by vibrating a finger in the water. ■ See how the waves spread out from the vibrating finger, in every direction in the water.

When a rubber band is stretched around a dish and plucked, the band vibrates. Is the rubber band vibrating *in* anything? Of course it is. The rubber band is vibrating *in air*.

AN INVESTIGATION into Waves

Needed: fifteen or more feet of clothes-line or other light rope

Tie one end of the rope to a firm support such as a chair leg. Hold the other end so that the rope hangs just above the floor. ■

Now flip your hand up and down quickly. You make a kind of half-loop in the rope. What happens to the loop? ● ▲

As you can see, the loop travels down the rope in a wave. Try sending a wave along the whole length of the rope.

Each time you flip the rope, the movement travels along the rope as a wave. You have made a **model** that helps us describe how sound travels. How would you explain what a model is? (After page 50, try to improve your explanation.) Are there other models in your classroom?

Additional Investigation: If you can get two drums, try this. Have someone beat one drum very hard. Stand close by with the other drum. Hold the tip of a finger lightly on the skin of the drum. What happens to your drum? How do you explain your result?

As the rubber band vibrates, it sends out waves in the air around it.■ Notice how the waves spread out in every direction. When these waves beat against your ear, you hear the sound of the vibrating rubber band.

When something vibrates in the air, it makes waves. The waves travel through the air.

Sound waves are carried by the air. If this is so, then taking away the air ■

ought to mean that no sound can be heard. Here is a way of doing just that. This electric bell is hanging inside a glass jar.● There is air in the jar. When the bell is turned on, it can be heard ringing inside the jar. What if the air is removed?

Now the pump connected to the jar is started. The pump takes the air out of the jar, little by little. As it does, the sound of the bell becomes softer and softer. Finally, the bell cannot be heard. No air means no sound waves.

When you call "Hi" to a friend, your vocal cords vibrate and make waves in the air. The air around you carries these sound waves to your friend's ear.

Bouncing Molecules

When a drummer hits his bass drum, a sound wave travels through the air. When a cricket chirps, sound waves travel through the air. When a tight rubber band is plucked, sound waves travel through the air. What happens to air when it carries a sound wave?

Air, you know, is made up of **molecules,** tiny specks of matter. The molecules in air are too small to see, even with the most powerful microscope. But let us imagine that we can see the molecules air is made of and that they look like tiny balls. What happens to them when a rubber band vibrates?

The rubber band swings to one side as it begins vibrating. It pushes against the air molecules on that side. ▲ The molecules are crowded together. They push against the molecules next to them. Those molecules push against the next ones. So the push travels along, from molecule to molecule. It travels away from the vibration that started it.

Now the rubber band swings back the other way. ◆ It leaves an empty space where it was. The molecules that have been pushed away rush back toward the rubber band. The molecules next to *them* rush back, and

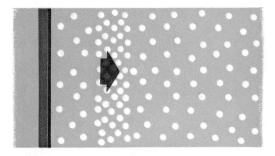

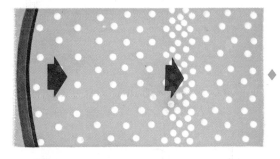

so the movement is passed along from molecule to molecule.

In this way the vibrations of the rubber band are passed along through the air from molecule to molecule. This movement of molecules, to and fro, is a **sound wave.** In the next section we shall learn more about the movement of molecules. Because of the molecules, sound travels through the air. Do you think that sound will travel through a solid—through iron or wood, for example? We shall investigate this question next.

BEFORE YOU GO ON Study these statements and choose the correct responses. Your study will help fix in your mind the main concept of this section.

1. When you hear the telephone ringing, sound waves are traveling to your ear through
    a. telephone wires   b. air

2. When a rubber band vibrates in air, it makes
    a. waves   b. molecules

3. When sound travels through air, the molecules in the air
    a. move to and fro   b. do not move

USING WHAT YOU KNOW On the Moon, where there is probably no air, two astronauts are walking one behind the other. The astronaut in back raps on his own helmet with his hand. Will the astronaut in front hear the rapping? Why?

ON YOUR OWN Use a coiled wire spring (Slinky) to show how waves travel. Show your model in class.

Can you think of a way to show how the pitch of a sound can be changed? For example, you might use glasses and water. If you do, try to explain the change in pitch.

4. Sound and Molecules

The idea that things about you are made up of molecules explains a lot. For instance, soon after a drop of perfume is put on a dish, perfume can be smelled in every part of a room. The idea of molecules explains this. We can imagine molecules of perfume leaving the drop on the dish, jumping into the air, and mixing with the molecules in the air. Since all the molecules are moving about and bumping into each other, the molecules of perfume soon travel to all parts of the room.

There are many other things that the idea of molecules helps to explain. Scientists call this kind of idea a **theory** (THEE·uh·ree). As you can see, a theory explains many different things that have been observed. The idea that things are made up of molecules is called the *molecular* (muh-LEK·yuh·lar) *theory*. Let us see what use we can make of the molecular theory, the theory that all the things about us are made up of molecules.

Using the Theory of Molecules

We used the molecular theory to explain how perfume spreads. Let us use this theory to explain something different.

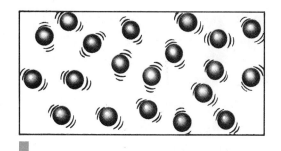

When you turn on a faucet, water pours out. Water is a **liquid.** Put some of this liquid in a tray, and put the tray in a freezer. In a while the water turns to ice. The liquid has become a **solid.** How is the solid different from the liquid?

Take some more liquid and put it in a pot. Heat it and let it boil. In a while the water boils away. It disappears because the water turns into an invisible **gas** and mixes with the air. Now the liquid has turned into a gas. How is the liquid different from the gas?

Water can be a solid. Water can be a liquid. Water can be a gas. What makes the difference? Let us see how the molecular theory explains the difference between a solid, a liquid, and a gas.

In a solid the molecules cannot move freely. Each molecule can move a little from side to side, but stays in its place. ■ Ordinarily, it cannot move away from the other molecules. A solid has a shape of its own.

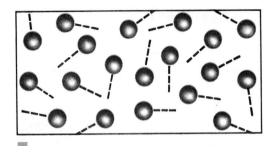

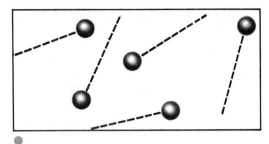

In a liquid the molecules can move more freely than in a solid. ■ And the molecules can slide over each other, like marbles poured from a bag.

In a gas the molecules are very far apart. ● Each molecule can move about freely.

This is how the molecular theory explains the difference between a solid, a liquid, and a gas.

Let us put the molecular theory to another test. Let us observe what happens when sound goes through a solid. Then we will see if the theory of molecules can explain what happens. Try the investigation on the opposite page. INVESTIGATE

The Theory Helps

A string telephone shows that the sound of a voice travels better through the solid string than through air. A pencil tapping on a wall shows that sound travels better through the solid wall than through air, which is a gas. Many investigations and ex-

periments have shown that sound does travel better through a solid than through a gas.

Why does sound travel better through a solid? Let us see if the molecular theory suggests why.

It is the to-and-fro movement of molecules that carries sound. Molecules bump their neighbors. The neighboring molecules pass on the bump to *their* neighbors, and so on. The molecules of a solid are close together. The molecules of a gas are far apart. Which molecules can bump each other more easily? Those that are close together, surely. If molecules bump more easily, they can carry sound better.

So the molecular theory does suggest an explanation. The theory is useful. This is what theories are for, and this is why scientists value theories so much. A good theory can explain many puzzles, in many different places. Because theories are so helpful, you will see the molecular theory used to explain other puzzles.

AN INVESTIGATION into Sound in a Gas and a Solid

Needed: about 10 feet of string, two paper cups, a wall, a pencil

Make a small hole in the bottom of each cup with the pencil point. Put one end of the string through the hole and knot the string so that it cannot come out. ■

Have a classmate hold one cup to his ear. Stretch the string tight, and whisper some numbers into the string telephone. ● Your classmate should repeat them aloud, to show that he has heard them. Then whisper some numbers without using the string telephone. Does your classmate hear them? Which carries sound better, the string or the air?

Put your ear against a wall. Have someone tap the wall from some distance away with the eraser end of a pencil. As the tapping goes on, lift your ear from the solid wall so that the sound reaches you through the air.

Which sound is louder, the one carried through the gas or the one carried through the solid?

Additional Investigation: Listen again to sounds through the string telephone. Let the string hang loose one time and stretch it tight the next. When does the

string carry sound better? How do you explain this?

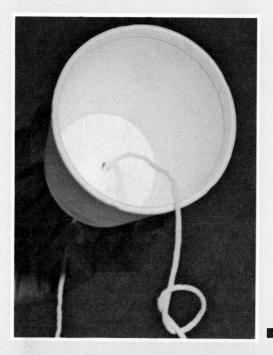
■

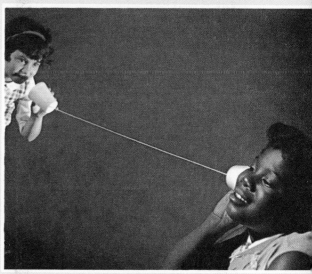
●

BEFORE
YOU GO ON Study these statements and choose the correct responses. Your study will help fix in your mind the main concept of this section.

1. An idea that explains many different things is called
   a. an investigation   b. a theory

2. According to the molecular theory, the molecules in a liquid
   a. are fixed in place   b. can slide over each other

3. Sound travels faster in a solid than in a gas because the molecules in a solid are
   a. closer together   b. farther apart

USING WHAT
YOU KNOW 1. An Indian would put his ear to the ground to hear distant horses. Why was this a good way to hear sounds?

2. Do you think that sound would travel faster in air or under water? Why?

5. When Sound Returns

This is a famous place in Zion National Park in the state of Utah. ■ If you call "Hello" across the valley, in a few seconds a ghostly voice will answer "Hello." "Who are you?" you call. Back comes the reply, "Who are you?" Whatever you call, the voice repeats exactly. You may notice that it replies in just the same tone, too. If you call out a long sentence, the voice will begin the reply before you have finished. It always repeats what you say. It is an **echo.**

Echoes are not found just anywhere, as you know. Why are echoes found in certain places? What makes an echo?

People who lived in Greece more than 2,500 years ago explained echoes this way. There was a girl named Echo, they said, who was in love with a certain young man. He did not love her, however, so she faded away until nothing was left but her voice. It is Echo, said the Greeks, who calls back.

We have kept the girl's name, as you see. However, we have a different explanation of what makes an echo.

Why Sound Returns

You shout "Hello!" ● Your vocal cords vibrate. Waves of sound come from your mouth and travel through the air. ▲ Some distance away is a brick wall. The sound waves hit the

▲

21

wall. What happens? The waves *bounce* off the wall. ■

Now the waves head back. ● In a short time the returning sound waves reach your ears. You hear "Hello" softly. It is an echo. ▲

An echo happens when sound waves bounce. What is across the valley in the picture on page 20? The hard stone wall of a steep cliff. So the sound waves of a "Hello" travel across the valley to the cliff. They bounce off the side of the mountain. They come back across the valley. The person who shouted hears an echo.

Remember that a sound wave is made up of molecules in the air moving forward and backward, to and fro. The mountain is made of mole- ●

cules, too. However, the stone in the mountain is a solid. Its molecules are packed close together. The molecules in the air are far apart. They bounce off the molecules of stone.

One thing that is needed for an echo, then, is something for sound to bounce off. If you could visit all the Echo Lakes and Echo Valleys and Echo Mountains in the world, you would be sure to find that each has a wall of some kind off which to bounce the sound and make the echo.

How Fast Is Sound

It takes more than a wall and a shout to make an echo, however. Perhaps there is a wall near you now. If you say "Hello" to it, you won't hear

an echo; and you still won't, even if you shout "Hello." Why not?

Let us go back to the cliff again for a moment. When you shout "Hello" there, it takes 6 or 8 seconds for the echo to return. In that time the sound waves travel across to the cliff, bounce, and come back. Do you see what this means? *It takes time for sound to travel* across the valley and back.

It takes time for sound to travel. Of course it does, now that you think of it. You hear the sound of the bat hitting the ball *after* you see it, when you are some distance away from the batter. It takes time for the sound waves to travel to you. Have you noticed that you can see a distant bass drummer hit his drum before you hear him? It takes time for sound waves to travel. It takes time for the bumping of molecules to pass along through air.

How much time does it take? After many investigations and experiments, scientists have measured the speed of sound. Sound travels about 1,100 feet in 1 second of time. That's about as long as four football fields.

If there is a watch or clock with a second hand nearby, count off some seconds. "One . . . two . . . three . . . four. . . ." When you are saying "two," how far has the sound of "one" traveled? It has sped about 1,100 feet away in that second of time. By the time you are saying "three," that first sound is $2 \times 1,100$ feet away, or 2,200 feet.

Suppose that the face of the cliff is exactly 1,100 feet away. How long will it take a "Hello" to get to the mountain? About 1 second. How long will it take that sound to come back? About 1 second. So the total time for the trip, going and returning, will be about 2 seconds.

If you say "Hello" to a wall close to you, the sound does bounce from the wall. But it goes to the wall and returns to you in so little time that

you may find the room noisy. You may wish that the sound did not bounce so much.

Now that we know what sound is and how it behaves, we can control it better. If we do not want the molecules of a sound wave to bounce off a wall, we hang soft curtains on the wall. The moving molecules in the air sink in among the molecules of cloth and do not bounce. We say that the cloth **absorbs** (ab·ZORBZ) the sound.

To absorb sound, the walls and ceiling of a noisy room may be covered with tiles like these. ■ Notice the holes in the tile. Molecules of air that hit where these holes are cannot do much bouncing. So the bounce of a sound wave is cut down by this sound-absorbing tile. The molecular theory is very useful when it comes to designing sound-absorbing materials like these.

you cannot make it out. You cannot hear an echo from a close wall, even though sound waves bounce from it.

Stopping the Bounce

You will not hear an echo when sound bounces from walls close to you. If there is a lot of sound, however, and it bounces from the walls,

BEFORE YOU GO ON Study these statements and choose the correct responses. Your study will help fix in your mind the main concept of this section.

1. An echo happens because sound waves
   a. can bounce off walls   b. cannot bounce off walls

2. Sound travels at a speed of about
   a. 1,100 feet a second   b. 1,100 feet a minute

3. When a sound wave hits a hard smooth wall, the wall
   a. absorbs the sound   b. bounces the sound back

USING WHAT
YOU KNOW 1. A builder wants to make a room that is soundproof. What do you suggest he do? Explain by using the molecular theory.

2. You see the flash of an exploding skyrocket in the night sky. Five seconds later you hear the bang. About how far away was the rocket?

6. The Main Concept: Sound and Molecules

What makes a sound?

We know that when we hear a sound, something is vibrating. We know that these vibrations are making waves in the air. We know the waves are traveling through the air to our ears from the thing that is vibrating. We know that when the vibration stops, the sound stops too.

What else have we found out about sound? The faster a thing vibrates, the higher the pitch of the sound. The slower the vibrations, the lower the pitch. A policeman's whistle makes a sound of high pitch. A tuba makes a low-pitched sound.

We know that sound travels through the air at about 1,100 feet in a second. Because it does, and be-

cause sound bounces off a hard surface, it can make an echo. We know that an echo is a sound that has traveled away from us and bounced back.

We know these things because we have been studying sound. Yet we have really been studying about how molecules behave.

The Movement of Molecules

When we hear a sound we know that something is vibrating and passing its vibrations to the air around it. Air is made up of molecules, however. It is the molecules in air that pick up the vibrations. It is the molecules in air that pass the vibrations along.

Molecules next to the vibrating object are pushed by the object as it vibrates. Those molecules push the molecules next to them. So the push is passed along from one molecule to the next. Each molecule moves back and forth in its place as it passes the vibration along. What if the molecules could not move? The sound would not be passed along. There would be no sound waves. If molecules did not bounce, there would be no echoes.

If molecules were not able to move fast or slowly, there would be no difference in pitch.

We have really been studying how molecules behave when something vibrates, even though we have never seen a molecule.

Fixing the Main Concepts

TESTING YOURSELF

Study the statements below and choose the correct responses. Your study will help fix in your mind the main concepts of this section.

1. The molecular theory helps us to explain
   a. sound   b. everything

2. A very fast vibration of a string results in a sound of
   a. high pitch   b. low pitch

3. A low-pitched sound is heard. The object making the sound must be vibrating
   a. rapidly   b. slowly

4. When you speak, your vocal cords are
   a. quiet   b. vibrating

5. A sound wave travels fastest in a
   a. gas   b. solid

6. An echo means that sound waves have
   a. bounced   b. been absorbed

7. When molecules carry sound, they
   a. disappear   b. move to and fro

8. It takes 2 seconds for a sound to come back from a wall. The wall is
   a. 1,100 feet away   b. 2,200 feet away

9. A wall with tiny holes in it is most likely to
   a. absorb sound   b. echo sound

10. Sound travels in solids more quickly than in gases because in solids the molecules are
    a. closer together than in gases
    b. farther apart than in gases

FOR YOUR READING

1. *High Sounds, Low Sounds,* by Franklyn M. Branley, published by Thomas Y. Crowell, New York, 1967. This book explains how vibrations arise, how they are carried to our ears, and how the vibrations produce sounds. The book suggests several investigations that you can readily do with materials found at home or in your classroom.

2. *How You Talk,* by Paul Showers, published by Thomas Y. Crowell, New York, 1966. This book's large, colorful pictures help you understand how your lips, tongue, teeth, and larynx work to produce sounds.

GOING FURTHER

1. Use your knowledge of sound to make a musical instrument out of eight pop bottles or water tumblers.

2. Use a funnel and rubber tube to invent a tool to listen to very soft sounds, like the tick of a watch. A doctor uses a tool that is something like that. What soft sounds does he hear with it? What is the name of the tool?

UNIT TWO

THE BOUNCE
OF LIGHT

Light.

You have only to close your eyes to know how important light is to you.

What is light?

You cannot taste it. You cannot smell it or touch it. You cannot hear it. You can only see it.

How can we possibly learn anything about such strange stuff? Turn the page and see.

1. When Do We See?

Have you ever walked along a road on a dark night? All of a sudden an automobile comes around a corner and you see the road lighted up in front of you. Why was it you saw telephone poles, trees, houses—everything along the roadside?

Let's look at another common example.

Have you ever used a flashlight to look for something in the dark? You move the ray of light around, and at last it strikes the thing you are looking for. "I see it," you say. When you want to see something, you shine a light on it. ■ See the picture marked with a square. But is just shining a light on something always enough to see it?

Here is the same figure, and the same light is shining on it.● The figure has been painted black. Though the light is shining on the figure, the figure can hardly be seen. Just shining a light on something you want to see is not enough, then. What else is needed? Try the investigation on the opposite page. You will find some evidence there. INVESTIGATE

When Light Hits

When the mirror is held in the light in front of the dark book, the page lights up brightly. Why? Because the

AN INVESTIGATION into How Light Behaves

Needed: a book, a mirror, a light, a piece of black paper, a piece of white paper

Open to a blank white page inside the front or back cover of the book. Prop the book against the light so that the open page is in a shadow, like this. ■

Hold the mirror in front of the book, toward the light. What happens to the dark page? ● Hold the white paper in front of the book, toward the light. What happens to the dark page? ▲

Now hold the black paper in front of the book, toward the light. What happens to the dark page now? ◆

How do you account for what happens each time?

Additional Investigation: Try different colors of papers in the same way. What happens to the dark page? Why?

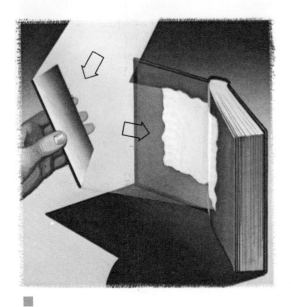

light that hits the mirror bounces off and hits the book. ■

You knew this long ago, to be sure. Haven't you bounced sunlight off a mirror to make a spot of light dash around a room? That spot showed something about light. It showed that *light bounces.*

What happens when light hits the white paper? When the paper is held in the light in front of the book, the book lights up. Light bounces from the white paper to the book.

When light bounces, it is said to be **reflected.** Light was reflected from the paper to the book. Light was reflected from the mirror to the book.

When the black paper is held in front of the book, almost no light bounces from it. ● Black paper does

not reflect light. Instead of bouncing, most of the light sinks into the black paper. The light is *absorbed.*

When light hits something, it may be either reflected or absorbed. Shine

light from a flashlight on something. The light is reflected from it and bounces *back to your eye.*▲ You can see the object when light is reflected from it.

Mirror and Paper

You can see yourself in a mirror. Yet you cannot see yourself in a piece of white paper. Why not, if both paper and mirror reflect light? What makes the difference?

Have you ever looked at paper under a microscope? Even the smoothest looking paper has a rough and uneven surface. Here is a photograph of the paper of this book seen through a microscope. ♦

Because the surface of the paper is rough, light that strikes it is re-

♦

flected in all directions.★ We say that the light is **diffused.**

The reflecting surface of a mirror is very smooth indeed. The smooth and even surface reflects light in an even, regular way.◈ The rays of light are

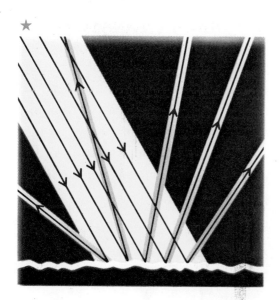

★

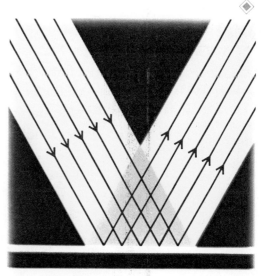

◈

not mixed up, as they are when reflected from a piece of paper—or another rough surface. You can see yourself in a mirror because the reflected light is regular. You cannot see yourself in a piece of paper because the reflected light is diffused. That is, the light is scattered in all directions.

BEFORE YOU GO ON Study these statements and choose the correct responses. Your study will help fix in your mind the main concept of this section.

1. When light hits a mirror, most of the light
   a. bounces   b. sinks in

2. When light hits a piece of black paper, most of the light is
   a. reflected   b. absorbed

3. White paper diffuses light because the paper is
   a. smooth   b. rough

4. You can see this page because light from it is being reflected
   a. away from your eyes   b. to your eyes

USING WHAT YOU KNOW You have to choose wall paint for two rooms. In the kitchen plenty of strong light is needed. In the living room soft light is needed.

What colors of paint would you choose? Why? You can also choose paints that will give a smooth finish or a rough finish. What kind of paint would you put on the walls of the kitchen? What kind would you put on the walls of the living room? Why?

ON YOUR OWN Does chalk dust absorb or reflect light? If your teacher permits, demonstrate this to your class.

2. Light and Sound

Most of the things we see, we see by reflected light. Light bounces from them to our eyes. Look around you. How many different things are reflecting light to your eyes now?

Yet there are some things that you do not see by reflected light. Some things make their own light. An electric light bulb makes its own light. A candle flame makes its own light. The television screen makes its own light. The Sun makes its own light. So do the other stars. (The Moon is seen by reflected light, as you probably know.)

Some things make their own light. Most things, however, are seen by reflected light.

Does the fact that light bounces remind you of sound? Sound bounces too. When we hear an echo, sound is being reflected and is bouncing back to our ears. Light and sound are alike in another way. Light can be absorbed instead of reflected. Sound can be absorbed too. When sound strikes a soft material, such as cloth, some of the sound may sink in, instead of being reflected.

Do sound and light behave alike in other ways? Let us observe another way that light behaves, and see.

The Path of Light

A straight tube of cardboard or newspaper, 2 or 3 feet long, will help you to find out more about light.

Look through the tube. You can see out the other end, because light rays are traveling through the tube to your eye. ■ Put the end of the tube to your ear. If someone speaks softly into the tube, you can hear the sound. Both light and sound can travel through the tube.

Now stuff a crumpled piece of paper into the tube. Of course you cannot see through the tube any longer. You can still hear through it, however. Sound can get through the crumpled

35

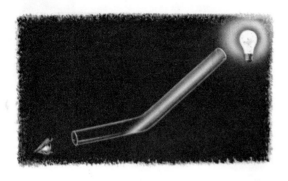

can still clearly hear sound through it. Sound is not stopped by the bend.

If a friend calls you from around a corner, you can *hear*. You cannot *see* your friend, though, because light travels in straight lines only. Sound travels in straight lines too. But sound can go around corners as well. ●

Where Light Can Travel

Light cannot travel around corners. Sound can. Sound can travel through substances that light cannot get through.

Yet light can travel where sound cannot. Light can travel through space where there are no molecules. Sound cannot. Light can travel through space from the Sun to the Earth, from the Sun to the Moon, from the Moon to the Earth. Light can travel through space from the stars to the Earth, and from the Earth to the Moon. Sound cannot.

Sound travels by molecules bumping each other, moving to and fro, passing along the push and pull of a vibrating object. Sound can travel through solids such as wood and iron, through liquids such as water, through gases such as air. Solids, liquids, and gases are all made up of molecules. For sound to travel, molecules are necessary. Where there are no mole-

paper all right. Light does not. Here, then, is one difference between light and sound. Sound can pass through some things that light cannot get through.

There is another difference between light and sound that is shown by this simple tube. Of course you know that if you bend the tube enough, you will not be able to see through it. Have you ever thought what this tells you about light? You cannot see through a tube that is not straight, because *light travels in straight lines only*. ■

What about sound? If you put the end of the bent tube to your ear, you cules, or too few, sound cannot travel. Astronauts landing on the Moon cannot talk to each other as they do on Earth. There is no air on the Moon, so there are no molecules of air to carry sound. There are so few molecules in space that sound cannot travel at all.

Molecules are necessary for sound to travel. Molecules are not necessary for light to travel, however. Light can travel where there are no molecules. Light can travel through space.

Light and sound behave alike in some ways, but they are not alike.

BEFORE YOU GO ON Study these statements and choose the correct responses. Your study will help fix in your mind the main concept of this section.

1. Sound and light are

    a. the same   b. different

2. Sound and light are aimed at a thin wooden door. The one that gets through is

    a. sound   b. light

3. Only one of these can travel through outer space. That one is

    a. sound   b. light

4. Molecules are necessary for one of these to travel. That one is

    a. sound   b. light

USING WHAT YOU KNOW

1. Explain how you would make a room soundproof.

2. How would you make a room lightproof? Why would your plan work?

ON YOUR OWN

Ask a builder for pieces of material used to cut down sound in a room. Take the material apart and see if you can explain how it works.

3. Bending Light

Heat goes with the Sun's light, you know. When you stay too long in the sunlight, the Sun's **energy** cooks your skin. You say you are sunburned, but it might be better to say sun-cooked.

Here is something that puts the Sun's energy to good use. ■ This sun cooker makes use of reflection. Light from the Sun is collected by the shiny surfaces and reflected to the container in the middle. Food can be cooked.

There is a way of collecting light that does not depend on reflection. Try it yourself. `INVESTIGATE`

AN INVESTIGATION into Light through a Lens

Needed: a magnifying glass (convex lens), a pie tin or metal plate, a piece of paper, a piece of cardboard, sunlight

A lens that is thicker in the middle than at the edges, like a magnifying glass, is called a convex lens. Hold the convex lens between the paper and the Sun, and facing the Sun.

Move the lens back and forth between the Sun and the paper until a small and bright spot of light rests on the paper. Hold the lens in that position. What happens to the paper? ■ What does this show about the spot of light?

Hold the lens between the sunlight and the cardboard. Move the cardboard first farther from the lens, then closer to it. ● ▲ As you move the cardboard back and forth, what happens to the spot of light on the cardboard?

Make a drawing of what happens to the light that goes through the convex lens to the cardboard.

Additional Investigation: Darken the room and shine a flashlight on the wall. Invent a way of using a lens to focus the light from the flashlight into a tiny, bright spot on the wall. Explain your results.

Purpose of a Lens

You may have used a magnifying glass or convex lens before. But have you ever thought about what the **lens** shows about light?

What is the lens doing when it makes that very bright and hot spot of light? The lens collects light from a large area and aims it at a small area. ■ We say the lens **focuses** the light when it brings the light to a point. The heat where the light is focused may be great enough to scorch or burn paper.

How does the lens focus light? The sun cooker focuses light by reflection.

How does the lens do it? The lens *bends* the light. ■

The light passing through the glass of the lens is bent, so that all of it meets at one place. Notice that the light that passes through the edge of the lens is bent the most. The light that passes near the center of the lens is bent only a little. The light at the center goes straight through.

What does the lens show us about light? It adds to our knowledge of light by showing us that *light can be bent.*

Do you know how the bending of light is important to you? Here is a

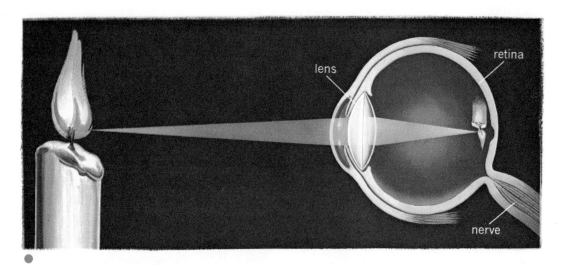

lens — retina — nerve

drawing of your eye. ● Notice the convex lens. It focuses light on the back of the eye, the **retina** (RET·ih-nuh). Light from an object must strike your retina for you to be able to see the object. Without a lens to bend the light entering your eye, you would not see clearly at all.

More Bending Light

Here is an aquarium with some water in it. A few drops of milk have been put in the water to make it cloudy so that light passing through the water can be seen. A beam of light is aimed at the water. What happens to the beam of light as it enters the water? ▲

A mirror has been laid at the bottom of the tank, under the water. What happens to the light when it strikes the mirror?

The mirror sends the beam of light up again, and out of the water. What happens to the light as it leaves the water? ▲

Here is another example of bending light that you can easily try for yourself. Put a coin in an empty saucer. Then get down so that the edge of the

▲

saucer just hides the coin from your eyes. Pour in water, slowly and carefully. The coin will slowly appear above the rim of the saucer. ■ See if you can figure out how the light goes from the coin to your eye. Make a drawing and then compare it with the rays on page 41. Light can be bent, but it is bent in a special way.

The rays of light from the coin to your eye are bent over the edge of the saucer like this.●

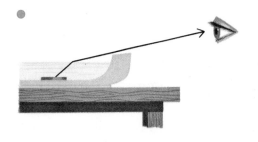

compare it with the rays on page 41.

BEFORE YOU GO ON Study these statements and choose the correct responses. Your study will help fix in your mind the main concept of this section.

1. When light is collected and brought to a point by a lens, we say the light is
    a. reflected   b. focused

2. Light going through a convex lens
    a. is bent   b. goes straight through

3. Light going through water
    a. may be bent   b. must go straight through

USING WHAT YOU KNOW If you had no lens in your eye, would you see light at all? Demonstrate your answer with a convex lens and a cardboard screen.

ON YOUR OWN Explain how this periscope works. ▲ Then see if you can explain how this one works. ◆

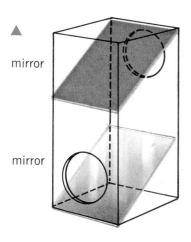

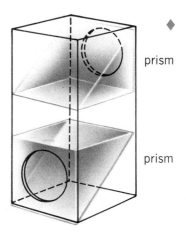

4. One Way to Make Light: A Candle

Look at what we have found out about light by observing how light behaves, by reasoning, and by using knowledge that scientists have given us.

Light travels in straight lines.
Light can be reflected.
Light can be absorbed.
Light can be bent.
Light can travel through space.

We have been able to find out something about this strange stuff, light, after all—even though we cannot feel light, taste it, smell it, or hear it.

What makes light?

Let us make some light with an old-fashioned light maker, a candle. It can show us something about how light is made.

A burning candle makes light and heat. At the same time, while it is making light and heat, what is happening to its paraffin (PAR·ah·fin)?

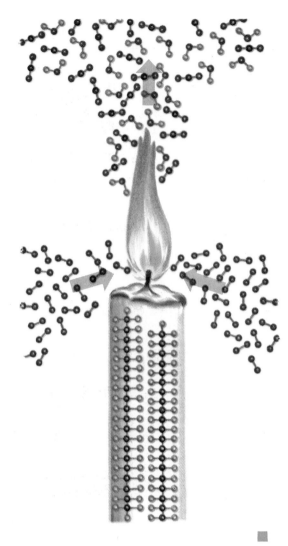

Molecules and Light

Like all matter, paraffin is made up of molecules. When you light the candle, you heat some of the paraffin. In the heat, the molecules that make up paraffin change into other molecules. (Some molecules from the air take part in these changes, as you will learn on page 121.) As the paraffin molecules change, they give off light and heat.

The new molecules that are formed scatter into the air around the candle. The substance of the candle disappears—not because it has been destroyed, but because it cannot be seen. Its molecules are scattered far and wide in the air. ■

A change in which new molecules form is a **chemical change.** Burning is a chemical change. If paper is burned, it changes to a substance very different from what it was. It changes into a black or gray ashy substance. The molecules that made up the paper have been through a chemical change.

Molecules of gasoline go through a chemical change when they burn in the engine of a car. Coal is changed chemically when it burns, as it gives off light and heat.

It is a chemical change in the molecules of the paraffin that causes a candle to give off light.

See for yourself by doing the investigation on the next page. INVESTIGATE

As you observe, some paraffin disappears as the candle burns. As the paraffin disappears, heat and light are given off, aren't they? Somehow, then, the lost paraffin seems connected with the light given off. But how?

AN INVESTIGATION
into Making Light

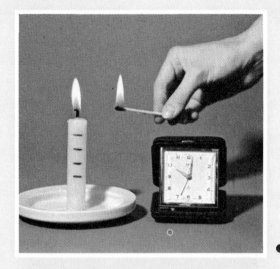

Needed: a candle, a ruler, a pencil, a candle holder, a clock or watch

Mark inches and half-inches on the candle with the pencil and ruler.■

Put the candle in the holder. Light the candle and write down the time.

Let the candle burn in a place where there are no drafts. Be sure that it is a safe place. The substance of the candle is paraffin. How long does it take for half an inch of the paraffin to disappear? How long does the next half-inch take to disappear?

What appears as the paraffin disappears? What do you think happens to the paraffin?

Here is what happened in one investigation.●▲♦ How can you explain the change that takes place?

Additional Investigation: How might a candle be used as a kind of clock?

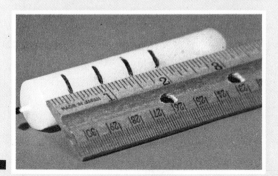

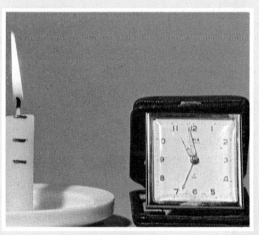

45

What the Changing Molecules Do

As a candle burns, a chemical change is taking place. The molecules in the paraffin are changing into other molecules. As they change, they make a flame that gives off light and heat. In other words, as the molecules change, they give off energy.

You eat food so that you will have energy and be able to do the things you want to do. When you wind up a clock, you are giving the clock energy so that it will go. Gasoline is useful because it has energy in it that will make an engine go. Energy, scientists say, is the ability to do work, to make matter move.

The paraffin of a candle contains energy. It is chemical energy. When the candle burns, its chemical energy is changed into light energy and heat energy. In other words, as the molecules in the paraffin change into other molecules, they give off light energy and heat energy. When we burn coal, or natural gas, or gasoline, the changing molecules give off energy that we can use.

As paraffin burns and gives off energy, its molecules are changed into other molecules. What other molecules does paraffin change to? See for yourself. Try the investigation on the opposite page. INVESTIGATE

The Chemical Change of a Candle

As the candle inside the jar burns, its molecules change into other molecules. A chemical change takes place.

What collects on the jar above the flame as the candle burns? Little drops gather on the glass. They are drops of water. When paraffin burns, molecules of water are formed.

What happens to the limewater as the candle burns? At the beginning, the limewater is clear. As the candle burns, however, the limewater becomes cloudy and white.

When clear limewater turns a white or milky color, it means just one thing. It means that carbon dioxide molecules have entered the limewater. Limewater turns milky when carbon dioxide is present.

The limewater in the jar turns a milky color as the candle burns, because carbon dioxide forms as a candle burns. Some of the molecules of paraffin are changed to molecules of carbon dioxide.

Thus the paraffin of the burning candle goes through a chemical change. The paraffin changes to water and carbon dioxide. As this chemical change takes place, the chemical energy of the paraffin in the candle changes. It changes into light energy and heat energy.

AN INVESTIGATION into a Chemical Change that Makes Light

Needed: two dry jars, a short candle, a piece of tape, limewater

Use melted wax to make the candle stick to one jar. Pour about an inch of clear limewater into the jar. ■

Light the candle. Carefully lower the second jar onto the mouth of the first. ● The candle will burn for a few moments. ▲ What do you see happen in the jar above the flame?

After the candle has gone out, tape the jars together without letting air in. Then shake them gently so that the limewater and the air in the jars are mixed. Here is one trial. ◆ What happens to the limewater? Why?

Additional Investigation: What substance is formed in the jar above the flame? Design an investigation to find out.

 ●

 ▲

 ■

 ◆

What makes the light of a candle? The answer is chemical energy. Molecules are rearranged to form other molecules. As this chemical change takes place, energy is given off. That is the story behind the common event we have been investigating, a candle burning.

BEFORE YOU GO ON Study these statements and choose the correct responses. Your study will help fix in your mind the main concept of this section.

1. The flame of a candle is made by
   a. molecules disappearing into the air
   b. molecules rearranging to form other molecules

2. In a chemical change, molecules
   a. do not change
   b. are rearranged to form other molecules

3. The light and heat of a candle come from
   a. chemical energy   b. unchanging molecules

4. A burning candle gives off water and
   a. carbon dioxide   b. nitrogen

5. How Light Travels

You flip a light switch. At once light reaches all parts of the room. You push the switch on a powerful flashlight. At once the beam hits the target, no matter how far away it is. Light seems to take no time at all to get somewhere. But light does take time to travel. Light travels so fast, however, that ordinarily we cannot notice the time. Light travels at the speed of *186,000 miles in one second.* Light does not take much time to cross your room, then, when you flip the switch. Just the same, it does take some time.

How does light travel?

The investigation on the opposite page will furnish some evidence to answer this question. INVESTIGATE

AN INVESTIGATION into How Light Travels

Needed: two pieces of polarized (POH-luh·riz'd) plastic or glass

Look through each piece of polarized plastic. Does light pass through it? Turn the piece, like this. ■ Does light still pass through? No matter how it is turned, light passes through it.

Now place one piece on the other, and look through both at one time. Turn one of the pieces, holding the other piece still. ● What happens as one of the pieces is turned? ▲ How can this behavior of light be explained?

Additional Investigation: Does polarized glass change light from a lamp? Design an investigation to find out.

How the Light Is Stopped

Light passes through each piece of **polarized** plastic, no matter how you turn the piece.

Yet when the two pieces are together in a certain position, light cannot get through them. In another position, light can get through.

What does this strange behavior mean about light? Scientists think that this behavior means that light travels in waves. Let us see why, with a **model.** Scientists make models in order to help themselves to understand things. They make models of airplanes and rockets, models of things you can see. However, scien-tists also make models of *ideas* they have. For example, scientists make models of atoms. They make models of things they need to explain.

Can we think of a model that behaves like light and polarized plastic?

Here is a chair, a rope passing through the back of the chair, and two boys. ■ One of the boys is sending waves along the rope by flipping the end. The waves pass right through the back of the chair, along the rope to the other boy.

Now another chair is placed in front of the first one. Even with two chairs, the waves along the rope pass through. ●

Now, however, one chair is turned this way. ▲ Now the chairs block the waves. No waves can pass through the second chair.

By turning the chair around still farther, waves can go through again. They can pass when the two backs are in line.

What does this model show us? It shows that there is a way of stopping *waves*, a way that works like the polarized plastic. It suggests to us that light is made up of waves. The way light behaves as it passes through polarized plastic makes us think that light travels in waves. When you switch on a light, perhaps waves of light rush out from the bulb in all directions.

Scientists have done many, many experiments which show light behaving as if it were made up of waves. But scientists have done other experiments which show light behaving as if it were made up of tiny *particles!*

▲

Is light made up of waves, or of particles, or of both? It is a mystery you will hear more about later. At this moment scientists have two explanations of how light behaves. Sometimes light acts as if it is made up of waves. At other times light acts as if it is made up of particles.

BEFORE YOU GO ON Study these statements and choose the correct responses. Your study will help fix in your mind the main concept of this section.

1. Light travels at the speed of

    a. 186,000 miles per second b. 186,000 miles per hour

2. The way light behaves with polarized plastic makes us think that light may be made up of

    a. waves   b. particles

3. Sometimes light behaves as if it were made up of

    a. particles   b. molecules

USING WHAT YOU KNOW

1. Suppose you wanted to shut out light from a room. How could you do it by using polarized plastic?

2. How are sound waves different from light waves?

6. The Main Concept: How Light Behaves

Can you look back and remember what your idea of light was before you began this unit? Surely you have learned some things about light that you did not know before. Surely you have an idea of light that is different from the one you had at first.

You know that light
—travels in straight lines
—can be reflected
—can be absorbed
—can be diffused
—can be bent
—behaves as waves sometimes
—behaves as particles sometimes.

To make light, we burned a candle. As it burned, the candle went through a chemical change. As it burned, it gave off heat and light. The chemical energy in the paraffin was changed into heat energy and light energy.

Do we have to burn something whenever we make light? No, indeed. For instance, striking two stones together can make a spark of light. The Sun's light is not the result of burning. Nothing is burning in a glowing electric lamp. But whatever the light, it takes energy to make it. Striking stones together takes energy. The Sun is using up energy. An electric lamp uses up energy as it glows.

It seems that to make light, one form of energy is changed to another. This is true whether the light comes from the Sun or whether it comes from striking two rocks together.

Energy can be changed from one form to another.

Fixing the Main Concepts

Study the statements below and choose the correct responses. Your study will help fix in your mind the main concepts of this section.

1. Light, like sound, can
   a. be reflected   b. go around corners

2. A black cloth
   a. absorbs light   b. bends light

3. A mirror is useful because it
   a. absorbs light   b. reflects light

4. A lens is useful because it
   a. absorbs light   b. bends light

5. The idea that light travels in waves explains what happens when light is stopped by
   a. polarized plastic   b. ordinary glass

6. When a lens focuses light, the light is being
   a. diffused   b. bent

7. At the back of your eyes is the
   a. retina   b. lens

8. Work by scientists shows that light can behave as if it were made of
   a. atoms and molecules   b. waves and particles

9. An explanation in science
   a. is always true   b. may change

10. Light is a form of
   a. energy   b. matter

FOR YOUR READING *Explorations in Science: A Book of Basic Experiments,* by Harry Milgrom, published by E. P. Dutton, New York, 1961. This book has investigations on both light and sound.

GOING FURTHER Compare the human eye with a camera. How are they the same? How are they different?

The Ways of the Scientist

Already, some of the ways of the scientist are yours. What are some of these ways, often called "methods" or "processes"?

Perhaps you no longer "jump to conclusions"—at least, most times. Perhaps, before reaching a conclusion, you have now begun to ask: What is the evidence for this conclusion? When you ask this, you are perhaps asking: Can we depend upon your evidence? How was the evidence collected? Has more than one investigator collected evidence like this?

And if there is no evidence for the conclusions, you have begun to ask: What are your observations? Have your observations been checked by others? For you have learned that it is not enough to make just *one* observation.

And if there are no observations or evidence, you probably have begun to ask: Well, what *are* your reasons for this conclusion?

No doubt, you have also begun to make your own observations. You have learned to keep records of your observations. You have also begun to read about what others have done. That is, before you investigate, you try to find out what is already known.

Then, too, you have begun to invent your own ways of investigating. You may even have begun to design your own experiments. Yes, you have begun to use the ways (or processes) of the scientist. Percy Bridgeman, a great scientist, a great investigator, called the ways of the scientist: *The Methods of Intelligence.* Why would he call them so?

A New View of Sound and Light

Your idea of what light and sound are like has changed from what it was. You have a new idea of what light and sound are like—a new **concept** of light and sound. What is a concept? It is something important and useful to you. Let us see why.

What Is a Concept?

Look at the animals on this page. ■ What sort of animal are they? You have no trouble recognizing them. They are all dogs, of course.

Here is something strange, however. Every one of these dogs is different. Perhaps there is a kind of dog here you have never seen before. Even so, you know it is a dog. How can you know what something is that you have never seen before? How do you know that all these different-looking animals are dogs?

You know that all these different animals are dogs because you have in your mind a *general idea* of what a dog looks like. You have put together this general idea of a dog from all the dogs you have seen. This general idea is called a concept. You have a concept of a dog in your mind. Because you have this concept, you can recognize dogs when you see them, even though they are different. Because you have a concept of a dog, you can recognize a dog even though you may never have seen that kind of dog before.

Here is another example of a concept. Use your imagination for a moment. How many different kinds of balls are used in games? ■ Big ones. Small ones. Different colors. Different materials. Baseballs, golf balls, rubber balls, basketballs. tennis balls, marbles, ball bearings, wooden balls, bowling balls. All different, yet you have a general idea of the way in which all these different balls are alike. You have a concept which helps you to recognize an object as a ball. It is built up from many observations.

Think for a moment and you will find that you have many different concepts in mind. Why? Because concepts are very useful things.

What Use Has a Concept?

It is hard to imagine such a thing, but suppose that you did not have a concept of what a ball is like. Every time you saw a kind of ball that you had not seen before, it would be something new.

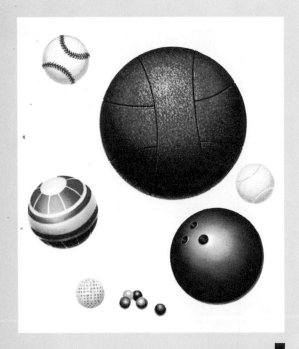

A concept brings together, or relates, a lot of different things that are somehow alike. Here is a basket of balls.● In what ways are they different? In what ways are they alike? A concept is like a basket in which you put certain things that are alike in some ways. Like a basket, a concept can collect together in one place many different things that are somehow related. Like a basket, a concept makes things easier to carry in your mind.

Here is another way in which a concept is useful. Imagine that you meet someone who has on a leash an animal you have never seen before. "What is it?" you say. "It's a kind of dog," the owner replies. "Oh," you say, "a dog!" Now, all at once you know a good deal about this strange animal. What you know about dogs in general holds good for this new one. Your concept of a dog has come to help you.

Concepts are useful because they bring together, or *relate*, things that would be scattered about in your mind. Concepts are useful because they help you to understand new, strange things. Concepts help make order out of disorder and help you to understand the world you live in. So concepts are especially important to scientists, who try for order and understanding of how the world works.

Light and Sound

You have a new concept now of light and of sound. These new concepts help you to understand light and sound. When you hear a sound, no matter what it is, you know that energy is being used to make something vibrate to and fro. The sound waves travel through the air to your ears. When you see a light, you know that energy is being used to make light waves that reach your eyes. When you see sunlight, you know that the light waves are traveling through space.

You know that sound and light both use energy. The sound of the starter's pistol at a race is heard because the chemical energy in the gunpowder is turned into sound energy. The light of a candle is seen because the chemical energy in the paraffin is changed into light energy.

When you hear music, some kind of energy is being changed into the energy of the moving air that makes up the sound wave. ■

When you turn on a flashlight, chemical energy changes to electric energy, which then changes to light energy. ●

Here, then, is another concept, one

that connects the concepts of light and sound. It is that energy can be changed from one form into another. Chemical energy can be changed into sound energy. Chemical energy can be changed into light energy and heat energy. The energy of movement can be changed into sound energy. The energy of electricity can be changed into light energy. Rub your hands together, hard. What is the energy of movement of your hands changed to? Heat energy, as you can feel. Clap your hands together. What is the energy of movement of your hands changed to now? To sound energy.

Energy can be changed from one form to another. Here is a concept that must connect many different things, for we live in a world of energy. You will hear more of it.

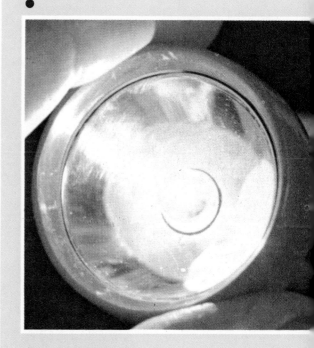

UNIT THREE

THE TRAVELS OF A DROP OF WATER

There are some things you must have to stay alive. One of these precious things is water.

You cannot live without water. Plants cannot live without water. Animals cannot live without water.

The drops of water you see on these leaves fell from the sky. How did they get up in the sky? What made them fall? What happened to them after they fell?

We can begin the travels of a drop of water by putting a drop of water back up in the sky.

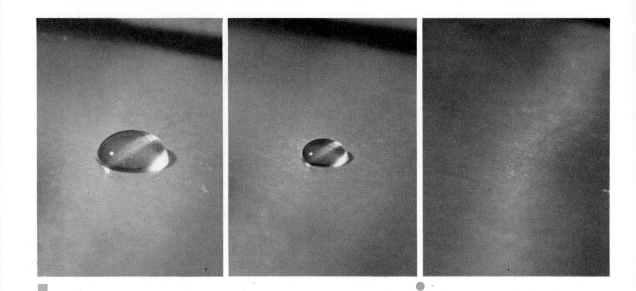

1. The Disappearing Drop of Water

Take a dry glass and put one drop of water in it. Put the glass in a warm place—in the sunlight or near a radiator. See the picture marked with a square. ■ Leave the drop of water there. In a while it disappears. ●

Isn't this disappearance rather strange? Water is a substance. You drink it, swim in it, float boats on it. Substances do not just disappear, usually. Yet water does.

Where does that disappearing drop go? You can answer this question by making another drop disappear and then appear again. See for yourself by doing the investigation on the opposite page. `INVESTIGATE`

How Water Behaves

Water can disappear and appear again. Let us see how.

Water is a substance. This means that water is made of those tiny bits of matter called molecules. You remember that there are molecules in the air and that they move back and forth when an object vibrates. A solid, too, is made of molecules that are packed tightly together. Sunlight also makes molecules move back and forth, and objects become hot. Any substance—solid, liquid, or gas—is made of molecules. Water, a liquid, is made of molecules, and they can be made to move.

Of course one molecule of water is very tiny. It cannot be seen. However, if a crowd of water molecules

AN INVESTIGATION into a Disappearing Drop of Water

Needed: two glasses, sticky tape, a medicine dropper, ice, water, bowl

Using the medicine dropper, put a drop of water in the bottom of one glass. Tape the two glasses together.■ The tape closes the opening so that nothing can enter or leave the glasses. You have a closed glass chamber with a drop of water in it.●

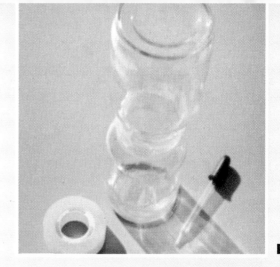

Let your glass chamber stand in a warm place, in sunlight or near a warm radiator. What happens to the drop of water in a few hours? Here is what happened in one trial.▲

The drop of water cannot be seen. It has disappeared. Yet it must be inside. It cannot pass through the glass or the tape around the glass.

Now stand the glass chamber in about an inch of ice water, in a bowl. In about 15 minutes, lift out the glass chamber and dry the outside. What do you see on the inside of the glass? Here is what happened in one trial.◆

Where did the water go when it disappeared? What made the water disappear? What made it return?

Additional Investigation: What happens to drops of water in an open glass if the glass is warmed, then cooled quickly?

63

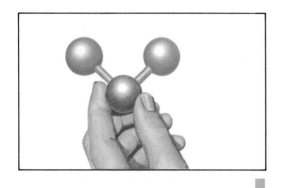

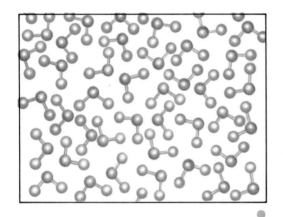

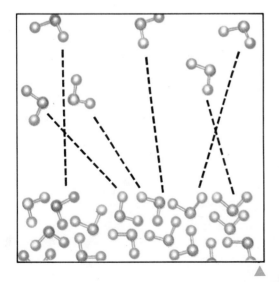

gathers, we can see the crowd. Let us imagine that a model of a molecule of water looks like this. ■ Then we can imagine that a drop of water might look like this. ●

When you put a drop of water in the glass chamber and the water disappears, here is what happens. A drop of water is a great crowd of water molecules. Some of these water molecules leave the crowd. They escape into the air. ▲ We say the water **evaporates.** The molecules of water mix with the air. As more and more water molecules leave, the drop gets smaller and smaller. In time all of the drop evaporates. All the water molecules go into the air.

Notice that all the water molecules are still inside the glass chamber. However, they are scattered in the air. They are far apart. The water has become an invisible gas. This invisible gas is **water vapor.** When you place the glass chamber in sunlight or near a warm radiator, the liquid water evaporates and becomes a gas—water vapor.

All the water molecules are still in the chamber, but they are no longer gathered together in a crowd. You cannot see them.

When you place the glass chamber in the refrigerator, the opposite happens. Water molecules come back out of the air and gather on the glass. They stop being a gas—water vapor. They become a liquid again—water. You can see the water. You can also taste it if you want to. Water molecules have come back together.

Water, it seems, can become an invisible gas, called water vapor. And this invisible gas can become visible water again. This you learned in your investigation. It will always happen every time you try it.

BEFORE YOU GO ON   Study these statements and choose the correct responses. Your study will help fix in your mind the main concept of this section.

1. Water vapor is a
   a. liquid   b. gas

2. When water evaporates, it turns into invisible
   a. water vapor   b. air

3. Compared with water, the molecules in water vapor are
   a. closer together   b. farther apart

USING WHAT YOU KNOW   1. A drop of water is placed in an *open* glass. The drop disappears after a time. What has happened to the molecules of water?

2. A drop of perfume on a plate soon disappears, but the perfume can be smelled in the air. What has happened?

ON YOUR OWN   Try to demonstrate that water evaporates faster in moving air than in still air.

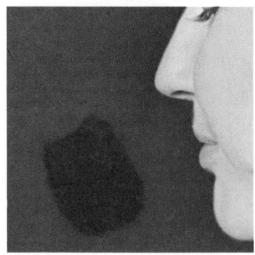

2. Water from the Air

Go to a chalkboard or a mirror and breathe on it. A damp spot appears. It is made by water in your breath. Watch what happens to the spot. It disappears. It evaporates as the molecules of water that make the spot fly out into the air. As it evaporates, liquid water changes to invisible gas —water vapor.

The same thing happens to drops of water, to puddles, to ponds, and to oceans. Molecules of water fly into the air from them. Since this is so, there must be many water molecules in the air around us. Can we catch some of them? Can we get some water from the air? See for yourself. Try the investigation on the opposite page. INVESTIGATE

Water in the Air

Suddenly, water appears on the outside of a shiny can. There is water inside the can, cold water. But the water on the outside does not come from inside the can. The water cannot pass through the side of the can.

The water that gathers on the outside of the shiny can *comes from the air* around the can. We have taken water from the air. Let us see how it happens. Perhaps you can make a good guess. Try to reason it out from what you know about molecules and how they behave.

When some ice is put into the can, the water in the can gets colder and colder. As the water gets colder, the can gets colder. And as the can gets colder, the air touching the can gets colder.

AN INVESTIGATION into Getting Water from the Air

Needed: an empty shiny can, ice, water

Remove the paper label from an empty can by soaking it. The surface of the can should be shiny. Dry the can. ■

Put water in the can until it is about half full. Do not get water on the outside of the can—keep the outside dry.

Now add some ice to the water in the can. As the ice is cooling the water, watch the shiny surface of the can carefully. ●

In a few moments, what happens to the shiny surface? Here is what happened in one trial. ▲

Touch the dull surface with your finger. ◆ It is water. Where did the water come from?

Additional Investigation: Predict what will happen to the water on the outside of the can when the water inside warms up again. Let the can of water warm up to test your prediction.

67

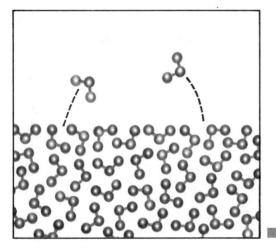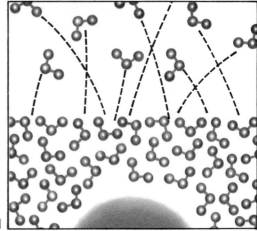

In the air around the can, there are molecules of water vapor. *As the air gets colder, it cannot hold so many molecules of water vapor.* Warm air can hold many molecules of water vapor. Cold air can hold only a few. So as the air next to the can gets colder, the air has to give up some of its water vapor molecules.

What happens to these water vapor molecules that are being pushed out of the air? The water vapor molecules become liquid water on the cold shiny side of the can.

You know what happens when a sponge full of water is squeezed. It cannot hold so much water. Some of the water comes out. When air is cooled, it cannot hold so much water vapor. Some of the water vapor comes out. The water vapor that comes out turns to liquid water.

When water vapor becomes liquid water, we say that the water vapor **condenses** (kon·DEN·sez). The water vapor condensed in the air around the cold, shiny can. As the air cooled, the water vapor in it condensed on the can and made a layer of water. **Condensation** took place.

Here is another example of condensation. When you breathe out, you breathe out water vapor. When you breathe on a chalkboard, the water vapor in your breath condenses on the board. This condensation makes a thin layer of water on the board.

Why does the water vapor in your breath condense on a chalkboard? The chalkboard is cooler than the warm air you breathe out. When the warm air touches the chalkboard, the air is cooled. Some of the water vapor condenses on the chalkboard.

There is water in the air around us. It got there by evaporation. We got back some of it by condensation.

It Takes Energy

Wet a finger. Hold it up and move it about in the air. Do you observe two things happening to your wet finger?

The finger dries, of course. The water evaporates. The water molecules fly off and become water vapor. There is something else, however. Did you notice that your finger becomes cool?

As the water evaporates, your finger becomes cool. Your finger becomes cool because it is *losing heat*. What is it losing heat to? Your finger is losing heat to the water that is evaporating. Evaporation takes heat energy. To go on, evaporation has to have heat energy. The water evaporating from your finger takes heat from your finger.

What is one way of getting water to evaporate quickly? Heat the water. Boiling water evaporates much more quickly than ice water. Warm water evaporates more quickly than cold water. Warm water has more heat energy than cold water. Evaporation takes heat energy.

Molecules are always on the move. Heat energy makes molecules move about more. The molecules can jump into the air faster and higher. More molecules can escape into the air. ■ Evaporation goes faster.

If some heat energy is taken away from these moving molecules, what will happen? The molecules will slow down. If enough heat energy is taken away, then water vapor molecules will slow down enough to become water again. The water vapor will condense. To make water vapor condense into water, heat energy must be taken away from the water vapor.

BEFORE YOU GO ON   Study these statements and choose the correct responses. Your study will help fix in your mind the main concept of this section.

1. Which one of these can hold more molecules of water?
   a. warm air   b. cold air

2. Water that is changing from liquid to gas is
   a. evaporating   b. condensing

3. Water vapor that is cooled enough
    a. evaporates   b. condenses

4. To evaporate, water needs
    a. heat energy   b. no energy

5. Heat energy makes molecules of water
    a. move faster   b. slow down

USING WHAT YOU KNOW

1. Fanning makes water on our skin evaporate. Why does fanning cool us?

2. Where does the water that collects on the outside of a glass of ice water come from? Why?

ON YOUR OWN

You know that water condenses on a can filled with ice. The temperature at which this condensation happens is called the *dew point*.

Is the dew point lower on a muggy day than on a dry day, or is it higher? How can you find out?

3. A Cloud Is Made

Have you ever watched clouds? Have you watched a cloud slowly change shape? Clouds seem to come in all shapes and sizes. Some look like feathers drifting across the sky. Some look like great lumps of cotton. Some are white, some are gray. Some are white on top and gray on the bottom.

Some clouds make a gray roof over our heads that shuts out the Sun. Sometimes there are no clouds at all.

Some clouds come with sunlight and warm weather. Some come with sunlight and cold weather. Some come with rain, some come with snow. Where do clouds come from? Where do they go? What are they made of? Let us think a bit first.

Pushing Molecules Apart

If you warm a balloon, it gets bigger. If you cool a balloon, it gets smaller. Why? Because of the *air* inside the balloon.

When air is warmed, it swells up. It takes up more space. We say that the air **expands**. When a balloon is warmed, the air inside the balloon is warmed. The air inside the balloon expands. The balloon gets bigger.

Air expands when it is heated. Remember that air is made up of molecules of different substances. These molecules are always on the move, bumping into each other, bouncing off each other. 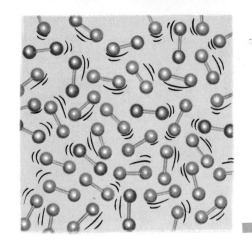 When they are heated, the molecules move faster, bump against each other harder, and push each other farther apart.

Air expands when it is heated because the molecules in the air move farther apart. What do you suppose happens when air is cooled, then? Just the opposite happens. When heat energy is taken away from air, the molecules slow down. They come closer together. They do not take up as much room as they did. Air takes up less space when it is cooled. We say that the air **contracts.**

When a balloon is cooled, the air in the balloon has heat energy taken away from it. The air contracts.

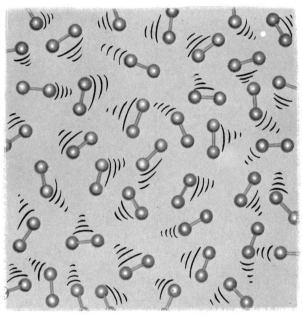

Air expands when heated and contracts when cooled. This is one step toward the making of a cloud. Knowing how air expands and contracts helps us to understand how clouds form. You can begin to find out more about clouds by doing the investigation on the next page. INVESTIGATE

AN INVESTIGATION into Warmed Air

Needed: two balloons, two pans, a bottle, a tape measure, hot and cold water

Put a few drops of water in the bottle. Put the balloon over the mouth of the bottle, like this. ■

Put some very hot water in a pan. Put the bottle in the water. ● What happens to the balloon? Here is what happened in one trial. ▲

How do you explain what happens? Put some cold water in the other pan. Place the bottle in the cold water. What happens to the balloon?

Here is what happened in one trial. ◆

An Additional Investigation: What will happen to the balloon on the bottle if the bottle is placed in sunlight? Predict what will happen and test your prediction.

●

▲

■

◆

Warm Air and Cold Air

Let us do an imaginary investigation. We will take two boxes that are really empty. They do not even have air in them. We will fill one with warm air and the other with cold air.

Which box has more molecules in it? Cold air molecules are closer together than warm air molecules. Then there must be more molecules in the box of cold air. ■

Which box weighs less, the one with the warm air or the one with the cold air? The box with fewer molecules in it weighs less, certainly. The box with the warm air weighs less than the box with the cold air. ●

Warm air is lighter than cold air. So warm air that is surrounded by cold air rises. You have seen evidence of this many times. Smoke rises from

a fire, doesn't it? Smoke is carried by warm air that is rising because the warm air is lighter than the cooler air around it. ▲

Warm air rises. This is another step toward the making of a cloud.

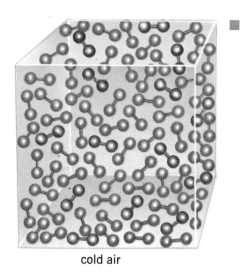

cold air

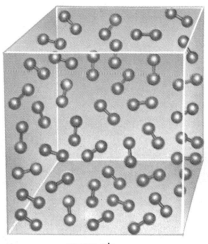

warm air

The Making of a Cloud

Which do you think is warmer on a hot day, a sandy beach or the water? If you have ever put your foot on hot sand, you know that the beach is warmer.

The beach is warmer than the water. This means that the air over the beach is warmer than the air over the water.

The warmer air over the beach rises. Up it goes, like invisible smoke, all along the hot beach. The warmer air rises because cooler air from over the water flows in and pushes it up. Of course, there is plenty of water vapor in this air from over the water. ■

The warm air over the beach rises. It goes miles high. As it rises, however,

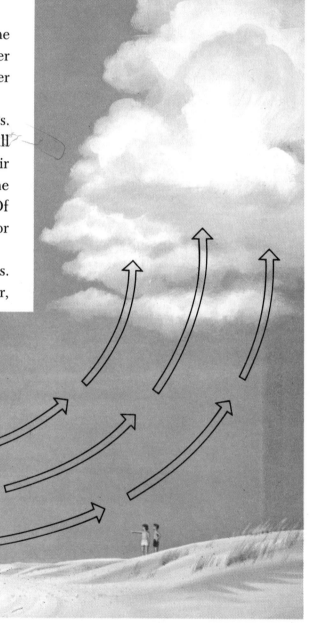

something happens to it. *The rising air cools.* The higher the rising air goes, the colder it gets.

Cold air cannot hold as much water vapor as warm air. The water vapor in this rising, cooling air condenses. It turns to water. The water vapor turns into tiny droplets of water, each one smaller than the point of a pin. These droplets form a cloud. A cloud is made up of tiny droplets of water, hanging in the air. A cloud is made from condensed water vapor.

You might wonder why these water droplets stay up in the sky. Remember that they are in rising air. The droplets are so small and light that the rising air can keep them from falling. Indeed, the rising air may sweep them up higher and build a towering cloud.

BEFORE YOU GO ON

Study these statements and choose the correct responses. Your study will help fix in your mind the main concept of this section.

1. Air that is heated
   a. contracts   b. expands

2. Warm air that is surrounded by cold air
   a. falls   b. rises

3. As air rises into the sky, the air gets
   a. colder   b. warmer

4. A cloud is formed when water vapor in rising air
   a. condenses   b. evaporates

USING WHAT YOU KNOW

1. Why don't clouds form easily over a desert?

2. On a damp day the smoke from a chimney may not rise far. Why?

ON YOUR OWN

How many kinds of clouds do you think there are? Look up "clouds" in an encyclopedia and see.

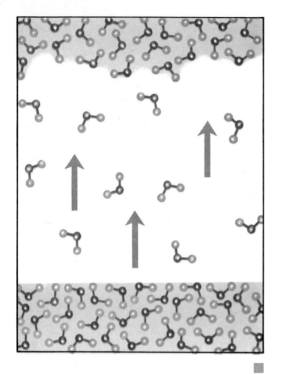

4. A Drop of Rain

What happens in a cloud to make it rain?

A cloud is a collection of tiny droplets of water. They are so tiny that it would take about one hundred of them side by side to reach across the head of a pin. If you have ever walked through fog, you know how the droplets in a cloud feel. Fog is a cloud down on the ground.

It takes about a million cloud droplets to make one raindrop. How do they get together? The investigation on the opposite page will suggest part of the answer. INVESTIGATE

Inside the Glass Chamber

What is happening in the glass chamber in the investigation? Something is happening, certainly. At the beginning of the investigation, the upper glass is clear. Little by little, a film of moisture collects on the clear glass. Water is collecting on the glass. Water is traveling from the bottom of the chamber to the top of the chamber, somehow.

How does water get from the bottom to the top of the glass chamber? At the bottom of the chamber, the water is evaporating. Water molecules are flying off the water. ■ They are becoming water vapor. Very soon the air in the chamber is full of water vapor.

At the top of the chamber, though, water vapor is condensing. The water vapor is turning into tiny droplets of water on the sides of the glass and is making the glass cloudy. The air at the top of the glass is cooler than the air at the bottom. So the water vapor at the top condenses. It forms tiny droplets.

Isn't this how a cloud is made? In a cloud, the air becomes cooler as it rises. In the glass chamber, the air cools as it reaches the top because it loses heat to the cooler part of the glass. In both the cloud and the glass

AN INVESTIGATION into a Glass of Water

Needed: two glasses, sticky tape, water

Pour some water into one glass. Tape the two glasses together, like this. ■ Make a tight seal with the tape so that nothing can get in or out of the glasses. Now you have a sealed glass chamber with water and air in it.

Put the glass chamber in a warm place. Notice that the upper part of the chamber is clear. ● Look at the chamber from time to time during the next hour or so. What happens to the upper part? Here is what happened in one trial. ▲ How can this be explained?

Additional Investigation: Try very wet soil instead of water. What happens this time in the chamber? Why?

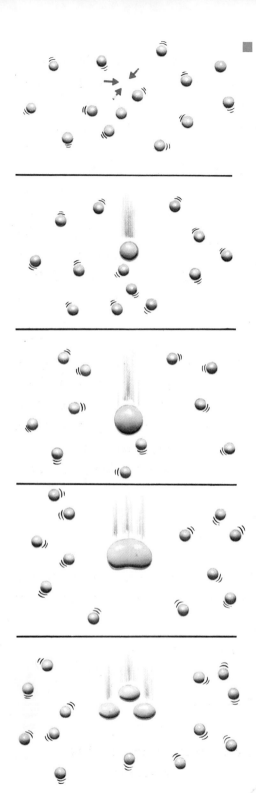

chamber, the same things happen. Air with water vapor in it rises and cools. The water vapor condenses into droplets. In the cloud, the droplets float in the air. In the glass chamber, the droplets gather on the glass to form larger drops.

The Droplets Grow

Something else happens in the glass chamber. At first the upper glass is only cloudy. There is only the thinnest layer of water on it. The droplets are too tiny to be seen. As time passes, however, more water condenses on the glass. You can begin to see drops of water on the glass. The drops get larger as the tiny droplets too small to be seen gather together to make bigger drops that can be seen.

Something like this happens in a cloud, too. The tiny droplets moving about in the rising air come together to make larger droplets. The larger droplet is heavier than the small ones. It starts to fall. As the larger droplet falls, it collides (bumps into) with more small droplets. These collisions make a large droplet larger still. It becomes a raindrop. ■

That is not the end, however. The raindrop may have still more collisions as it falls. It may get still bigger, so big that it cannot go on as one raindrop. It breaks into smaller drops. Each of these smaller drops now has collisions with droplets, and starts growing. It is a kind of chain reaction. One drop leads to others, and others, and still others.

At last some drops fall out of the cloud and fall to the ground. It is raining.

Unfinished Business

There is another way in which cloud droplets may come together to make raindrops. The droplets may be carried so high by the rising air that they are turned to crystals of ice.

The air has to be very cold for this freezing to happen. These crystals of ice get larger and larger. As they get larger, they get heavier and begin to fall through the cloud.

As they fall, the crystals of ice get into warmer air. If the air is warm enough, they melt and become raindrops. If the air is not warm enough, the crystals fall to the ground without melting. "It's snowing!" we say.

Scientists used to think that this was the only way in which clouds made rain. Then they found out that many clouds make rain without being cold enough to freeze the cloud droplets. Now scientists think that the collision of droplets must be important. But there is some unfinished business here. Just how do the very first tiny droplets come together to make a drop? How can enough collisions happen? Scientists are not yet sure of the answers to these questions.

Scientists are working on them, though.

BEFORE YOU GO ON Study these statements and choose the correct responses. Your study will help fix in your mind the main concept of this section.

1. A fog, like a cloud, is made up of
   a. water vapor   b. water droplets

2. To form a cloud, water vapor is
   a. evaporated   b. condensed

3. Raindrops are formed by small water droplets
   a. colliding   b. separating

ON YOUR OWN   Cloud seeding is supposed to help in forming rain. Do some library research. Find out how cloud seeding works. Does it produce rain?

5. Rivers in the Sea

Do you remember putting water in the bottom of a glass some time ago? The water disappeared. Where is that water now? Of course it evaporated. Its molecules flew off into the air and became a gas—water vapor. Where are those molecules now?

Many things may have happened to them. Perhaps those same molecules are still water vapor but are now being carried by the wind to far-off lands. Perhaps those molecules have condensed. Perhaps they are part of a cloud hundreds of miles away. ■ Or they may be falling somewhere as raindrops. Perhaps they have fallen somewhere on a mountain or in a valley. It may be that they are flowing down a river to the sea. They may be moving along in a great river in the sea. Yes, there are great rivers, or **currents,** in the sea. For example, there is one current in the sea called the Gulf Stream. Its light-colored water is warmer than the darker water through which it flows. It flows through the darker water like a great river, many miles wide.

What makes this warm current in the sea? The investigation on the opposite page will give an important clue to the answer. **INVESTIGATE**

■

AN INVESTIGATION into Mixing Cold and Warm Water

Needed: two large jars, two small bottles, ice water, warm water, red and blue ink

Fill one large jar and one small bottle with ice water. Add blue ink to the small bottle to color the water.

Fill the other large jar and small bottle with warm water. Add a few drops of red ink to the small bottle of warm water.

Take the bottle of blue ice water. Hold it just over the jar of warm water. ■ Slowly tilt the bottle. Let the cold blue water flow out into the warm water.● What happens to the cold water in the warm water?

Here is what happened in one trial. ▲

In the same way, empty the bottle of warm red water into the jar of cold water. What happens to warm water in the cold water? Here is what happened in one trial. ◆

How can you explain what happened?

Additional Investigation: Try the same investigation, using salt water. Are the results the same as in fresh water?

Sink or Float

When cold water is placed in warm water, the cold water sinks. When warm water is placed in cold water, the warm water rises.

Does this remind you of something? When warm air is in cold air, the warm air rises and the cold air sinks. This happens because warm air is lighter than cold air. The molecules of warm air are farther apart than molecules of cold air. This makes warm air weigh less than cold air.

Warm water is lighter than cold water, for the same reason. Warm water floats on top of cold water, then, if they are not mixed. The warm water in the Gulf Stream that has

come from the Gulf of Mexico floats on the cold water below it.

There is another reason why the water in the Gulf Stream is light and floats. Much rain falls in the Gulf of

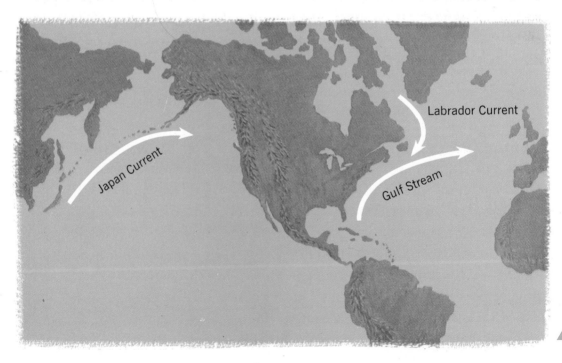

Mexico. Rainwater is lighter than seawater. Seawater contains many **dissolved** substances, which makes it heavy. Here is the amount of dissolved substances in a pailful of seawater. ■ Compare it with the amount of dissolved substances in a pailful of rainwater. ●

We saw that the light, warm water in the Gulf of Mexico does not stay there. It leaves the Gulf and flows along our Atlantic coast. ▲

Why does the Gulf Stream flow? The water is moved by wind. Wind blowing over water moves the top layer of water along.

Scientists are not yet sure just how wind moves water along, although they know that it happens. The fact that the Earth is turning while the water is being moved along affects

the path of the Gulf Stream too. It is not a simple problem, but wind is the main mover of the warm Gulf Stream.

A drop of rain that falls into the Gulf of Mexico may be carried into the Atlantic in this river of warm water. There are other currents in the sea that can carry a drop of water far. Notice the Japan Current. ▲ It is warm water, like the Gulf Stream. The Japanese call it Kuroshio (kur-o·SHE·o). Kuroshio means "black stream." This warm water is darker than the cold water around it.

The Labrador Current brings cold water from the north. It may bring icebergs as well. An iceberg may come from another kind of river, a river of ice called a **glacier** (GLAY·shur). Here is a glacier in Alaska. ◆ This glacier is a stream of ice that is slowly moving down this valley to the sea. The glacier is fed by snow in the mountains. As the river of ice reaches the sea, pieces of ice break off and float in the water. They are icebergs, which are slowly carried out to sea by ocean currents. In time they melt and turn to water.

The molecules of the drop of water you evaporated a while ago may be sliding down to the sea in a glacier, some time in the future. Perhaps they will become part of Kuroshio. Perhaps they are now part of the water vapor in the air you are taking into your lungs.

BEFORE YOU GO ON Study these statements and choose the correct responses. Your study will help fix in your mind the main concept of this section.

1. Warm water that is in cold water
   a. rises   b. falls

2. Compared with rainwater, seawater is
   a. lighter   b. heavier

3. A glacier is a slow-moving river of
   a. water   b. ice

4. The Gulf Stream is a warm current that moves on the
   a. top of the sea   b. bottom of the sea

5. The Gulf Stream is moved by the
   a. wind   b. water

USING WHAT YOU KNOW The Kuroshio, a current, probably has less salt in it than does the sea around it. Why?

6. The Water We Eat

If you squeeze all the juice from an orange, most of what you squeeze out will be water. All plants have water in them. All animals have water in them. All living things are made partly of water.

Living things must have water. This means you, too. You need water every so often. You cannot store water like a camel or a cactus.

One way you get water is by eating it. When you eat most foods, whether they are vegetables, eggs, meat, milk, apples, or potatoes, you eat the water in them.

Most plants take in water, which then becomes part of them. When animals eat the plants, the animals get the water in the plant. The water that plants and animals get comes usually from drops of water which fall from clouds. Let us see how water gets into an apple.

The Water in an Apple

Apples have plenty of water in them. About four-fifths of an apple may be water. Other foods have water in them too, so you get some of the water you need by eating.

How did the water get into the apple? Let us follow another drop of

water on a journey. This drop is one that falls near an apple tree in the middle of a summer shower.

The drop falls on the ground beside the tree. The drop does not stay on the top of the soil, however. It sinks into the soil, and slowly flows downward through the tiny spaces in the soil.

As the water moves down through the soil, it meets substances that are in the soil. The water dissolves some of these substances. The dissolved substances are carried along with the water, as it moves downward.

A few inches below the ground, the water meets one of the small roots of the apple tree. ■ The root has rootlets growing from it. Each rootlet has millions of hairs growing on it called **root hairs.** Root hairs are the means by which a plant takes in water. The water that has traveled through the soil enters the root hairs. The dissolved substances in the water enter too, along with the water.

Then the water and the substances in it travel up into the branches and leaves and fruit of the tree, through water tubes. The tree uses the dissolved substances in the water to grow and to make apples. Thus water enters the apples.

Most plants get water much the same way as the apple tree does. This is true of vegetables as well as fruits. You eat the fruits or vegetables and

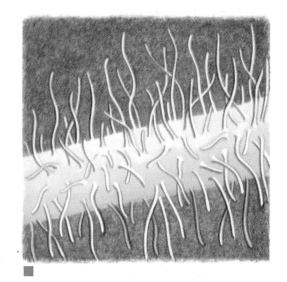

■

the water that has become part of them.

Is there much water in these foods? Let us find out for one of these foods from a growing plant, an apple. See for yourself. Try the investigation on the opposite page. INVESTIGATE

BEFORE YOU GO ON   Study these statements and choose the correct responses. Your study will help fix in your mind the main concept of this section.

1. The water we eat is found in
   a. most foods   b. plants only

2. Water entering the roots of plants
   a. has dissolved substances in it
   b. is pure rainwater

3. Most plants take in water through
   a. root hairs   b. water tubes

AN INVESTIGATION
into Water We Eat

Needed: an apple, a knife, a scale, a plastic bag, a paper towel, a tray.

Weigh the apple on the scale. ■ Copy the table below into your notebook and enter the weight of the apple in it. Here is the weight in one trial.

Cut the apple into small pieces. It will dry out more quickly this way. Put the pieces of apple on the paper towel on the tray. Place the tray in sunlight on a windowsill. ● Leave it there for several days. Water will evaporate from the pieces of apple.

Weigh the dried-out pieces of apple. ▲ Enter the weight in your science notebook, in a table like the one below. Calculate the weight of water lost by the apple.

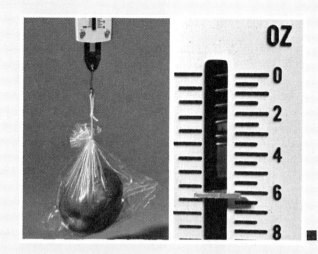

Weight of apple	_____
Weight of apple after drying	_____
Weight lost by apple	_____
Weight of water in apple	_____

Were the pieces of "dried-out" apple really dry? Can you think of another way of doing this investigation?

Additional Investigation: Find out how much water a potato has.

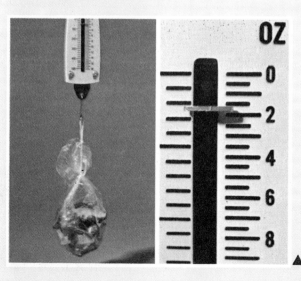

7. The Water We Drink

Here is a strange sight to most of us. These men are water carriers.  They sell drinking water. In their country, Morocco, water is so scarce that it can be sold like this.

When we are thirsty, we can go to a faucet or a well and drink as much as we want. We bathe, and we water growing plants. Each of us has to drink from six to eight glasses of water every day, besides the water we eat. Without water, we could not live. Without water, all plants and animals would die, sooner or later. Our water supply is most important. How do we get water?

Of course, water falls as rain and fills our rivers and lakes. Yet the water we drink is clean and pure. How do we clean our water? Try one way by doing the investigation on the opposite page. **INVESTIGATE**

Making Water Clean and Pure

The water that comes from a faucet in a big city like New York or Los Angeles comes from many miles away. New York's water supply begins with rain that falls in mountains many miles away from the city. Some of the water in Los Angeles comes from mountains in other states. As rain falls, the streams and rivers over a large area of land collect the rain. The area in which the streams and rivers collect the rain and snow is

88

Making a Model:
A Water-Purifying Plant

Needed: a funnel, sand, cotton, about half an inch of garden soil in a quart jar, another clean quart jar

Add about a quart of water to the jar with soil in it, and shake it up so that the water is full of soil particles. ■ Let the water stand for a while. What happens to the soil particles? ● What happens to the water as the particles settle to the bottom? Settling is one way of cleaning water.

Another way to clean water is to pass it through a filter of sand. The holes between the particles of sand are very small. Particles of soil are filtered out of the water passing through the sand.

Place cotton in the funnel, and put a layer of sand about an inch deep over the cotton. Put the funnel in the clean jar. Gently pour some water from the settling jar into the funnel. ▲ What will happen to the water in the funnel?

Additional Investigation: How does rainwater differ from soilwater? Invent a way of showing the difference.

■

●

▲

89

called a **watershed.** Sometimes dams are built in a watershed, and the water is stored in **reservoirs.**

The water in a reservoir does not move much, so some of the particles of soil and rock in the water have a chance to settle to the bottom. Then the water goes to a purifying plant.

In the purifying plant, the water is placed in a settling tank. ■ Substances are added to the water to make particles settle more quickly. Then the water is filtered through layers of sand. Now the water looks clean, but in it there may still be tiny invisible plants called **bacteria** that can make persons ill. So the water is sprayed into the air. Bacteria will be killed and the toxic gases will be removed by the air. Finally, a tiny amount of chlorine gas is added to the water to kill any bacteria left. The water is then fit to drink.

On the Farm or Ranch

It is fine to have reservoirs and purifying plants, but this does not help the farmer or rancher who does not live near a city water supply. How does he get water? From a well, you might say. What kind of a well?

One kind of well depends on water that sinks into the soil. In making such a well, the farmer really digs a deep, round hole in the ground. He lines its walls with rock to keep the soil from falling in. Water seeps in through the bottom and fills part of the well. To understand how such a well works, make a model. Take an aquarium and fill it partly with sand. This will be the soil surrounding the well. Make a round hole in the soil. In it place a tin can from which both ends have been removed. This tin can open at both ends will be the sides of the well. Sink it into the soil but not to the bottom of the aquarium. ●

What happens as water is poured on the soil outside the can? Try it first by filling the aquarium half way with water. How high does the water reach in the can? What happens as more water is added?

You can see that the water level in the well depends on the water level in the soil.

Heavy rainfall, or a large supply of water in the soil, raises the water level, or **water table,** in the soil. Light rainfall, or a small supply of water in the soil, lowers the water table. This

windmill pumps water from below the water table to the surface. ▲

Such a well is risky, isn't it? It depends on rainfall, or underground water. In dry weather, the well may dry up.

Some types of rock can also hold water. The next page shows such a rock layer. ■ High up on the hill, rainwater enters this rock. But the rainwater cannot leave the rock, for

▲

the rock lies between other layers through which water cannot move. The well driller sinks a metal pipe down into the water-carrying rock. The water rises in the pipe.

A drop of water may start in a cloud. It may end in the most unexpected places. You can have many adventures just by following the journeys of one drop of water!

BEFORE YOU GO ON Study these statements and choose the correct responses. Your study will help fix in your mind the main concept of this section.

1. The area in which the streams and rivers collect rainfall is called a
    a. reservoir   b. watershed

2. Bacteria in water are killed by spraying the water into the air and adding
    a. particles   b. chlorine

3. A water supply for some wells depends on the
    a. depth of the   b. width of the well
        water table

1. Why is it important to keep watersheds clean and safe?

2. What kind of well must be dug in a dry region? Why?

8. The Main Concept: Around and Around

A drop of water makes many different journeys. It flows down a river into a lake. There it leaves the ground and rises into the air, as water vapor. Up rise its molecules. They make a cloud. Presently the water droplets in the cloud form drops. Down comes a raindrop. It falls on the ground, sinks into the soil, and meets the roots of a tree. It is taken into the tree, carried up the trunk, into a branch, and then into a leaf. It is given off into the air by the leaf, as water vapor.

Again, the water vapor rises in the air. Again it forms cloud droplets. This time the droplets freeze and fall as snow. The snowflakes land on a cold mountaintop and slide down into a river of ice, a glacier. An iceberg breaks off the glacier, floats out to sea, and melts. The drop rises again to form another cloud.

This story has no end, has it? Molecules of water just go on traveling, on more different journeys than we can imagine.

Yet no matter how different the journeys that water molecules make, we know how they make them. Water evaporates. It turns to water vapor. The water vapor condenses and turns to water. Then the water evaporates. It turns to water vapor. Again the water vapor condenses and turns to water. This has no end either. Let us make a diagram that has no end, like this. ● No matter where you start, one happening leads to the next and the next and the next.

Since it goes around and around, this process is called a cycle. Since it is about water, it is called the **water cycle.**

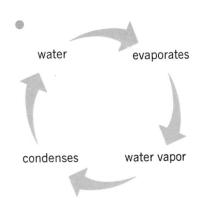

93

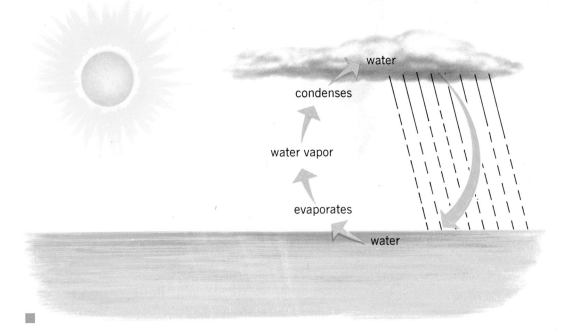

The water cycle will fit any journey that a drop of water can make. Here is an example. ■

You can see that molecules of water are used over and over again in the water cycle.

Energy for the Cycle

It takes energy to make a motorcycle go. The energy is supplied by gasoline. It takes energy to make a bicycle go. You supply the energy yourself.

It takes energy to make the water cycle go. After all, a water molecule has weight, even if it is a very small weight. To lift any weight takes energy. To lift billions of water molecules into the air to make a cloud takes a great deal of energy. Where does the energy come from? The Sun.

The Sun is the source of energy for the water cycle. It is the Sun that provides the energy for evaporation. The Sun heats the molecules of water on the surface. The heat energy that comes from the Sun makes the water molecules move faster. They zig-zag about, and bump against each other more often. The molecules at the surface of the water leap higher into the air. Most of these leaping molecules fall back again. But as the water becomes warmer, more molecules escape and become water vapor.

The travels of every drop of water, its rising into the air and falling back to the earth, depend on the Sun and gravity.

Fixing the Main Concepts

Study these statements and choose the correct responses. Your study will help fix in your mind the main concepts of this section.

1. Water vapor is made up of
   a. molecules   b. tiny droplets of water

2. Water vapor is a
   a. gas   b. liquid

3. When water evaporates, it becomes
   a. visible   b. invisible

4. When water vapor forms clouds, it
   a. evaporates   b. condenses

5. One box is filled with water. Another box, the same size and weight, is filled with water vapor. Which of the two boxes weighs less?
   a. the box of water vapor   b. the box of water

6. A box is filled with cold air. Another box, like the first, is filled with warm air. Which box weighs more?
   a. the box of warm air   b. the box of cold air

7. Warm air surrounded by cold air
   a. rises   b. sinks

8. Cold water surrounded by warm water
   a. rises   b. sinks

9. The water you eat in plants comes to us through the
   a. soil   b. reservoir

10. The water we drink is collected mainly in
    a. watersheds   b. water-carrying rock

FOR YOUR
READING

1. *Junior Science Book of Water Experiments*, by Rocco V. Feravolo, published by Garrard Press, New York, 1965. The author uses the word "experiment" in the same way the word "investigation" is used in your science book. The book's many investigations will help you understand the water cycle.

2. *Not Only for Ducks: The Story of Rain*, by Glenn O. Blough, published by McGraw-Hill, New York, 1954. A simple story of the water cycle is told in this book.

3. *Water, Our Vital Need*, by Walter Buehr, published by W. W. Norton, New York, 1967. This book tells how we get and protect our water supply.

ON YOUR OWN

What part of your refrigerator is coldest? What is your guess? If you remember what happened to warm and cold water when mixed, in the investigation on page 81, you may be able to make a good guess. Here is one way in which you can get some evidence to show how nearly right or wrong your guess is. A refrigerator, a thermometer, a watch, and pencil and paper are needed.

Make a copy of the diagram of the refrigerator shown on the next page. How many shelves are there in your refrigerator? On your diagram, put in as many places for thermometer readings as there are shelves.

Put the thermometer on the top shelf of your refrigerator, in about the center. Close the refrigerator door quickly. Leave the thermometer inside for about three minutes.

Open the door quickly. Read the temperature on the thermometer at once. Record this temperature reading on your refrigerator diagram. Place the thermometer in the middle of the second shelf from the top, and close the door. Keep the refrigerator door closed for three minutes. Then, open the door, read the thermometer, record the reading, move the thermometer down a shelf, and close the door again.

Don't let the thermometer touch the side of the refrigerator. Don't put the thermometer in a container.

In this way, you can obtain some evidence of the temperature at different levels in your refrigerator. Does the evidence confirm your guess about which part of the refrigerator is coldest?

Would the temperature readings be different if they were taken near the back wall of the refrigerator, instead of the middle? How would you find out?

refrigerator

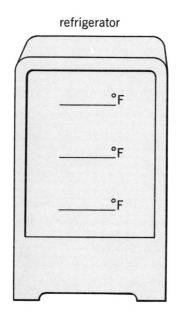

UNIT FOUR

THE TRAVELS OF SOME MOLECULES

What do you see in this picture?

You see boys and girls and green plants, of course. There is something else in this picture, however. It surrounds the boys and girls and the green plants. It cannot be seen, yet you know it must be there. It is invisible, but it can be felt. It is air.

There is a connection among the three things in the picture, among people and air and green plants.

People breathe air, to be sure. There is a connection. What do green plants have to do with people and air? That is what this unit is about.

We begin with a bottle of air.

1. A Bottle of Air

If you were asked to collect a bottle of air, how would you do it? Perhaps you think that getting a bottle of air is easy. It is, isn't it?

There is air all around us. What we call an "empty" bottle is already filled with air. To get a bottle of air is not hard.

What we want, however, is not just a bottle of air. We want a bottle of *clean* air. We need a bottle of air that has none of the dust and dirt that air usually carries. Dust and dirt are solids, tiny solid specks. How can we get a bottle of clean air free from the dust and dirt and other solids that are usually there?

There is a simple way of getting a bottle of air that is free from solids. Try the investigation opposite to see how it's done. INVESTIGATE

Collecting Gases

Air is a substance. Anything that is a substance takes up space. Air takes up space.

Water is a substance, too, and takes up space. What happens when air enters the bottle of water in the investigation? Two substances cannot be in the same space at the same time. As air is pushed into the bottle, water is pushed out. The air takes the place of the water, or **displaces** the water. As air displaces water in the bottle, you can see it happening, even though air is invisible. See the picture marked with a square. ■ This way of collecting air is called the **displacement method.**

As air is collecting in the bottle, it passes through the water. As the bubbles rise through the water, the air in the bubbles is washed clean. Any solids in the air are washed out by the water. So the bubbles that rise to the surface of the water inside the bottle hold clean air. The result is a bottle of air without solids in it.

The displacement method is one way to collect a gas. There is a problem in collecting a gas in this way, though.

Imagine you are watching ammonia gas being collected by the displacement method.

AN INVESTIGATION into a Way of Collecting Clean Air

Needed: a plastic bag, a plastic or rubber tube, a square of hard plastic, a small bottle, a pan, tape, and water

Put about 2 inches of water in the pan. Fill the bottle until it overflows.

Put the square of plastic over the mouth of the bottle so that no air gets in. Now there is only water in the bottle.

Hold the plastic tight and turn the bottle upside down. Place the mouth of the bottle under the water in the pan. ■ Remove the plastic, keeping the mouth of the bottle underwater. The water in the bottle will not run out.

Now open the plastic bag wide, so that there is plenty of air in it. Tape the bag of air to one end of the tube. ●

Put the other end of the tube under the water into the mouth of the bottle. Do not let the mouth of the bottle come out of the water. ▲ Press the bag. Air is squeezed out. Where does it go? How do you know? Here is what happened in one trial. ◆

What happens to the water in the bottle as air is squeezed out of the bag? Why? How does the air that is squeezed out of the bag get cleaned?

Additional Investigation: Blow air through the tube instead of squeezing air out of the bag. Will the air you collect now be different? Why?

Although the ammonia gas has been going into the bottle of water for some time, no gas has collected. Something strange happens to the bubbles. They get smaller and disappear as they rise. The problem is easily answered if you know this fact. Ammonia gas dissolves easily in water.

Air does not dissolve easily in water, as you can see. But a tiny bit of the air passing through the water does dissolve in the water. Water can hold some dissolved air. You have often seen evidence of this, although you may not have known it. What do you suppose the bubbles are that rise when you heat water?

BEFORE YOU GO ON Study these statements and choose the correct responses. Your study will help fix in your mind the main concept of this section.

1. An "empty" bottle open to the air is
   a. empty   b. not empty

2. When air is bubbled into the bottle of water, the air
   a. displaces the water   b. dissolves the water

3. A gas that cannot be collected by displacing water is
   a. ammonia   b. air

USING WHAT YOU KNOW The air coming into a hospital should be clean. What would be one way to clean the air?

ON YOUR OWN Invent a way to show that air has weight.

2. A Bottle of Oxygen

Now we have a way of collecting gases. Let us collect some oxygen gas for an investigation.

Where can we get oxygen? There is plenty of oxygen in the air around us, of course. Air not only has oxygen in it but other gases as well. Air is a mixture of gases.

All of the gases in air are well mixed together. Suppose that you could count out ten thousand molecules of air. The chances are that you would find these molecules among those ten thousand:

Substance	Number of Molecules
Nitrogen gas	7,800
Oxygen gas	2,100
Argon gas	90
Carbon dioxide	4
Other gases	6
Total	10,000

The air around you has a good deal of oxygen in it, as you can see. Separating molecules of oxygen from other molecules in the air is difficult, however. Special and expensive equipment is needed to do that job. Fortunately, there is another way which we can use for getting oxygen.

We can take a molecule that has oxygen in it as one of its parts. We can then break this molecule apart and take the oxygen.

Breaking Apart a Molecule

Many different kinds of molecules have oxygen as a part. Which kind of molecule shall we use? There is a substance called *hydrogen peroxide* (HY-droh·jen per·OK·syd). Hydrogen peroxide has oxygen in it, for it is made up of hydrogen and oxygen.

How can we take apart molecules of hydrogen peroxide and get the oxygen? We can do this with yeast. ■ When hydrogen peroxide touches yeast, the hydrogen peroxide comes apart and gives off oxygen. See for yourself in the investigation on the next page. Then, with the oxygen collected, investigate a difference between oxygen and air. INVESTIGATE

AN INVESTIGATION into Oxygen and Air

Needed: hydrogen peroxide, yeast powder, steel wool, two test tubes, two tumblers

With a pencil, push a wad of steel wool down to the bottom of each test tube. Put just a pinch of yeast powder into one of the test tubes.

Fill both tumblers with water. Fill the test tube with no yeast in it with water to the very brim. Put your thumb over the mouth of the tube and close it tight. Turn the test tube upside down. Put its mouth under the water in one

of the tumblers, keeping your thumb in place. ■ When the mouth of the tube is completely under water, take your thumb off. The water in the test tube will stay up in the tube.

Now fill the test tube with yeast in it to the brim with hydrogen peroxide. Quickly put your thumb over the end of the tube, closing it tight. Quickly turn the tube upside down and put the mouth under water in the second tumbler. Remove your thumb.

Watch the bubbles of gas collect in the top of the tube. The gas is oxygen. As the gas collects, the water in the tube is displaced.

Let out some of the water in the test tube with no yeast in it, so that the steel wool is in air rather than in

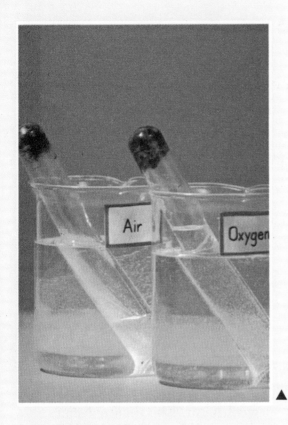

water. Now you have a piece of wet steel wool in air, in one tube. A piece of wet steel wool in oxygen is in the other tube.●

Observe the steel wool from time to time during the next few days. What happens to the steel wool in oxygen? In air?

Here is what happened in one trial.▲

Additional Investigation: Perhaps it is the yeast which is responsible for what has happened. Perhaps it is not the oxygen. How would you find out whether it is the oxygen or the yeast which causes the rusting?

Pure Oxygen and Air

Why does one piece of steel wool rust more quickly than the other, in the investigation?

To answer this question we must ask another question. What is happening when steel wool rusts?

Steel is mostly iron. It is the iron that rusts. What happens is that oxygen acts on the iron. When oxygen acts on iron, oxygen molecules and iron molecules come together. They form a new substance called *iron oxide*. We say that the oxygen **combines** with the iron to form iron oxide. Another name for iron oxide is rust.

Molecules of iron combine with molecules of oxygen. They form a new substance that is not like either iron or oxygen. A chemist might write

iron + oxygen ⟶ iron oxide

The arrow stands for "becomes." The plus sign stands for "combined with."

Now let us go back to our first question. Why does one piece of steel wool rust more quickly than the other, in the investigation?

Try thinking out your own answer to this question, before going on.

More Oxygen

In the investigation, one piece of steel wool was in air. The other piece

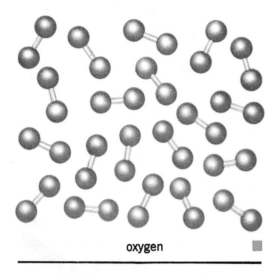

oxygen

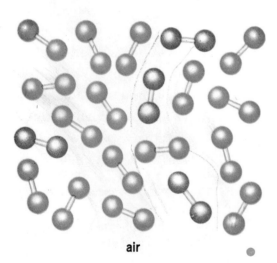

air

of steel wool was in oxygen. Both pieces rusted. However, the piece of steel wool in oxygen rusted more quickly than the piece in air. Why?

When steel wool rusts, molecules of oxygen combine with molecules of iron. Both the pieces of steel wool in the investigation had molecules of oxygen around them. The steel wool in oxygen was surrounded only by oxygen molecules. ■ The steel wool in air had some molecules of oxygen around it, for air contains molecules of oxygen. Air, however, is a mixture of gases. It has other molecules in it besides oxygen.● The steel wool in pure oxygen had many more molecules of oxygen around it than the steel wool in air. The iron molecules in the oxygen had many more chances to combine with oxygen molecules than the iron molecules in air.

BEFORE YOU GO ON Study these statements and choose the correct responses. This will help fix in your mind the main concept.

1. Air is mostly
   a. nitrogen gas   b. oxygen gas

2. Hydrogen peroxide is made of hydrogen and
   a. nitrogen   b. oxygen

3. When iron rusts, it combines with
   a. nitrogen   b. oxygen

1. Tools are sometimes stored in heavy oil. Why?

2. Would it be better if the air were made up of oxygen only? Why?

Where in your house do you find iron oxide?

3. Moving Molecules Around

We have moved some oxygen molecules around, haven't we? First, they were in hydrogen peroxide. We let them loose by using yeast. Then we tied up those oxygen molecules in rust. We combined oxygen molecules and iron molecules to make a new substance, iron oxide.

When you stop to think of it, being able to let loose or to join up molecules is a remarkable thing.

Let us look more closely at how this remarkable thing happens.

One Substance

Suppose that you could divide oxygen into smaller and smaller parts. Could you go on dividing forever? No. The smallest part which would *still be oxygen* would be a **molecule**—a molecule of oxygen.

It would be made up of two **atoms,** atoms of oxygen. ▲ If you divided that

molecule of oxygen further, you would no longer have oxygen. One atom of oxygen does not act like oxygen. A molecule with two atoms of oxygen does act like oxygen.

A molecule of oxygen is made up of two atoms of oxygen joined together. A molecule of oxygen is made up of just one kind of atom, atoms of oxygen. A substance that is made up

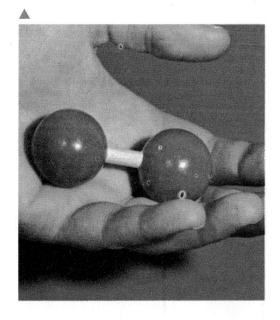

107

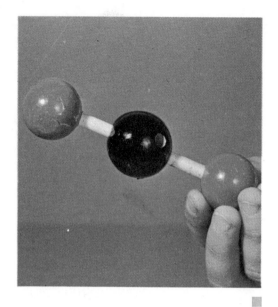

oxide would be a molecule. A molecule of carbon dioxide, though, is made up of *two* kinds of atoms, atoms of carbon and atoms of oxygen. ■

A molecule of carbon dioxide is made up of two different elements, then, carbon and oxygen. A substance made up of atoms of two or more different elements is called a **compound.** Carbon dioxide is a compound.

You know many compounds. Water is a compound of the elements hydrogen and oxygen. ●

Sugar is a compound with three elements combined in it. Sugar has the elements carbon, hydrogen, and oxygen combined in it. ▲

A compound may have more than two different elements combined in it.

of just one kind of atom is called an **element**. Oxygen is an element because every molecule has only atoms of oxygen in it. Copper is an element. A molecule has only atoms of copper in it. Molecules of copper cannot be divided into anything smaller and still be copper. Iron is an element, for it has only one kind of atom in it. Nitrogen is an element. The nitrogen molecule is made up only of nitrogen atoms. So nitrogen is an element.

Carbon dioxide, however, is *not* an element. Let us see why.

More Than One Kind

Suppose you could divide carbon dioxide gas into smaller and smaller parts. The smallest part of carbon di-

Elements and Compounds

An element is made up of only one kind of atom. Elements may be joined together, or combined, to make a compound. A compound is made up of more than one element. A compound may be broken apart into elements. This is what we were doing when we moved those molecules of oxygen around. We began with a bottle of hydrogen peroxide. Hydrogen peroxide is a compound that has two elements, hydrogen and oxygen, combined in it. By putting yeast in hydrogen peroxide we let the oxygen loose. The oxygen came loose as a gas, which we collected.

We put the oxygen together with iron. The molecules of oxygen and the molecules of iron combined. They formed another compound, iron oxide.

Thus we took an element from a compound, combined it with another element, and made a new compound. We moved oxygen molecules around and gave them new neighbors. We let loose some molecules and joined up some molecules.

BEFORE YOU GO ON Study these statements and choose the correct responses. Your study will help fix in your mind the main concept of this section.

1. All substances are made up of
   a. other substances   b. molecules

2. When a molecule is made up of only one kind of atom, it is
   a. an element   b. a compound

3. When a molecule is made up of two or more elements, it is

    a. an element   b. a compound

USING WHAT YOU KNOW
A red substance is heated. It gives off oxygen and mercury. The substance must be either an element or a compound. Which do you think it is? Why?

ON YOUR OWN
What elements and compounds can you find in your home?

4. The Rising Water

Let us move molecules of oxygen around in still another way.

Take a glass of water and an empty medicine dropper. Put the tip of the

dropper under water and squeeze the bulb. ■ What happens? Bubbles of air come from the dropper. The "empty" medicine dropper was full of air, of course. When the bulb is squeezed, air is pushed out. There is nothing mysterious about that.

What happens next really is a little mysterious, though. Keep the tip of the dropper under water. Gently let the bulb swell up again. What happens in the dropper?●

As the bulb swells up, water rises in the dropper. How can you explain this?

The Push of Air

Water rises in the medicine dropper when the rubber bulb is released. "The water is sucked up," someone may say. But water is not really sucked up. It is *pushed* up. Something is pushing the water up into the dropper. What is this something?

You probably know that the air around you is pressing on everything it touches, all the time. We say that the air has **pressure.** A good way to show that this is so is with a paper bag. Put your hand in the bag and push its sides out as far as they will go. Now you have a bag full of air. ▲

Now take some air out of the bag by sucking. ◆ What happens to the bag? It crumples up, as if you had pressed it with your hands. It is the pressure of the air outside the bag that crumples it. When air is taken out of the bag, the pressure inside the bag becomes smaller than the pressure outside. The air outside pushes the sides of the bag in. The air has pressure.

Why does the water rise in the medicine dropper? When the bulb is squeezed, air is pushed out of the dropper. (You saw the bubbles.) So when the bulb is allowed to swell up

▲

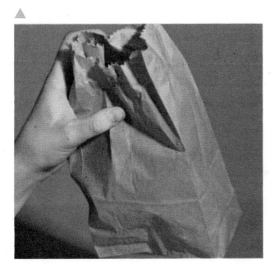

◆

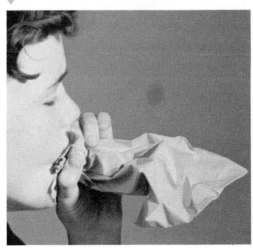

again, there is less air in the dropper. This means that the pressure of the air left in the dropper is less than the pressure of the air outside. The pressure outside the dropper then pushes water into the dropper. The water rises. ■

The water rises because some air has been taken out. With this in mind you may be able to solve the puzzle of some disappearing molecules. See for yourself by doing the investigation on the opposite page. INVESTIGATE

Something Is Missing

As the steel wool rusts in the test tube, in the investigation, the level of the water rises in the test tube. ●

Why does the water rise in the test tube? Remember why the water rose in the medicine dropper. Part of the air in the dropper was taken out. Water rose in the dropper to take the place of the air taken out.

Water rises in the test tube for the same reason. Part of the air in the test tube has been taken out. *Some of the molecules have disappeared from inside the test tube.*

Where have these missing molecules gone? We will follow the trail of the missing molecules next. Before we do, however, try a little detective work on your own. What do you think has happened to the missing molecules of air?

AN INVESTIGATION into Disappearing Molecules

Needed: a wad of steel wool, a large test tube, a pan of water, a marking pencil

Push the wad of steel wool to the bottom of the test tube. Do not pack the steel wool tightly, for air must be able to reach all parts of it. ■

Fill the test tube with water, then empty it. This will wet the steel wool and the inside of the test tube.

Place the test tube upside down in the pan of water. ●

Leave the test tube in the pan of water for several days. Observe what happens to the steel wool and to the level of the water in the test tube. Mark the level of the water each day.

Here is what happened during one trial. ▲

What happens to the steel wool? What happens to the water level? What happens to the amount of air inside the test tube? How do you explain what happens?

Additional Investigation: One boy used a steel-wool pad with soap in it for this investigation. Do you think his results were the same as with plain steel wool? Why do you think so? Design an investigation to test your prediction.

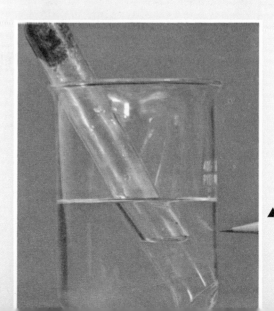

BEFORE
YOU GO ON Study these statements and choose the correct responses. Your study will help fix in your mind the main concept of this section.

1. A medicine dropper is squeezed in water. Then it is released. Water goes up into the medicine dropper because the water is

  a. sucked up   b. pushed up

2. As the steel wool rusts in the test tube (in the investigation), the water rises in the test tube. The water rises because the air in the test tube is

  a. increasing   b. getting less

USING WHAT
YOU KNOW Fill a test tube with water. Put your thumb tightly over the mouth of the tube. Put the mouth under water and take your thumb away. Why doesn't the water run out of the tube?

ON YOUR OWN **1.** Air has a pressure of about 14.7 pounds per square inch. What does this mean? Why does air have this pressure? Does it have this same pressure on a high mountain?

2. A book that uses helpful pictures to introduce you to concepts of matter is *Take a Balloon,* by A. Harris Stone and Bertram M. Siegal, published by Prentice-Hall, New York, 1967.

5. Finding the Missing Molecules

Steel wool rusts inside a test tube. As the steel wool rusts, the water rises. This shows that part of the air around the steel wool is being removed. Somehow, molecules of air are disappearing.

Rusting and molecules disappearing seem to be happening at the same time. Are rusting and disappearing molecules connected? Let us do some reasoning.

We know that rusting takes oxygen. When steel wool rusts, the iron in the steel wool combines with oxygen.■

We know that air has oxygen in it. Air is a mixture of gases. One of the gases is oxygen.

Perhaps the rusting is taking molecules of oxygen from the air in the test tube. This sounds like a good guess.

But how good is a guess?

A Scientist's Guess

What good is a guess? Scientists often make use of guesses. Their guesses are a special kind, however, and have a special name. A scientist may call his guess a **hypothesis** (hy-POTH·eh·sis). A hypothesis is a *possible* explanation for something observed.

What is the difference between a hypothesis and an ordinary guess? It is this. When we say hypothesis instead of guess, it means that we intend to *test* our explanation. We intend to look for evidence that our possible explanation is right or wrong. In science we must test our explanations.

We guess that rusting is taking oxygen from the air in the test tube. Let us call this guess a hypothesis. We have a hypothesis that rusting is taking oxygen from the air in the test tube.

Now let us look for some evidence that this hypothesis is right or wrong. Let us see if we can **confirm,** or prove, our hypothesis.

$\dfrac{1}{5}$

other four fifths is made up of other gases.

Our hypothesis, or explanation, is that rusting is taking oxygen from the air in the test tube. If our hypothesis is right, how much of the air can rusting take? No more than one fifth, for only one fifth of the air is oxygen.

One fifth of the air in the test tube is missing every time we do the investigation. If rusting is taking oxygen from the air, this is what we would expect. Here is some evidence to confirm our hypothesis.

One Fifth Is Missing

As the steel wool rusts in the test tube, the water rises. The water stops rising, however. It remains at one level. Did you observe this? The steel wool is not completely rusted, yet the water stops rising.

At this time, when the water has stopped rising, we can make another observation. Suppose we compare the height of the lost air with the height of the air to begin with. About one fifth of the air has been lost. ■ As often as this investigation is repeated, we will find that one fifth of the air has gone.

Do you happen to remember what part of the air is oxygen? One fifth of the air around us is oxygen. The

Another Check

Let us look for some more evidence for or against our hypothesis.

Suppose that all the oxygen in the test tube *has* been used up by the rusting of the steel wool. Would you expect a candle to burn in the air left in the test tube? No, for a candle must have oxygen to burn.

Here is a glass cylinder in which steel wool has rusted and the water has risen. A square of plastic is held tightly on the end under water, and the cylinder is turned right side up. No air from outside has got in. ●

Our hypothesis is that this cylinder has no oxygen in it. Now a lighted candle on a wire is lowered into the cylinder. What happens? ▲

The candle goes out at once. The candle behaves as if there is no oxygen in the cylinder.

Perhaps a lighted candle would not burn in such a cylinder, even if there were oxygen in the air? If a candle is lowered into ordinary air in the cylinder, it does not go out at once. It burns for a little while.

Here is more evidence to confirm our hypothesis, then. Because of this evidence, it seems more likely that our hypothesis is right, that rusting takes oxygen from the air in the test tube.

Does this evidence *prove* that our hypothesis is right? No. Scientists would ask for much more evidence than this. However, many other investigations have been done by scientists. A great deal of evidence has been collected. The evidence shows that the hypothesis is right. The rusting steel wool takes oxygen from the air.

The rusting steel wool takes oxygen molecules from the air. These oxygen molecules are combined with the iron in the steel wool. Thus the air has fewer molecules in it. The amount of air gets less.

You can see how useful a hypothesis may be. A scientist uses a hypothesis to find evidence. You can see, too, how useful a guess may be. A guess may lead to a hypothesis. Then the hypothesis may lead to a better explanation of what it is that puzzles the scientist. Or you.

Of course, sometimes a hypothesis turns out to be wrong. This doesn't always mean that it was a waste of time. A hypothesis that turns out to be wrong may help a scientist to find evidence for a correct hypothesis.

Study these statements and choose the correct responses. Your study will help fix in your mind the main concept of this section.

1. A scientist may guess at a possible explanation of what he sees. This possible explanation is a
    a. conclusion   b. hypothesis

2. When the rusting steel wool in the cylinder has used up all the oxygen, the water should rise
    a. one fifth of the way   b. four fifths of the way

3. A scientist uses a hypothesis
    a. to find more evidence   b. instead of evidence

Scientists are exploring the Moon. From what they know of the Moon, their hypothesis is that there is no life on the Moon similar to that on Earth.

Could their hypothesis be wrong? Or is a hypothesis always right?

Would you like to know more about the chemist's language? These books will help you get started: *The True Book of Chemistry,* by Philip Carona, published by Childrens Press, Chicago, 1963; *Chemistry: First S-T-E-P-S,* by Keith Gordon Irwin, published by Franklin Watts, 1963.

6. The Uses of Oxygen

Think for a moment about how important oxygen is.

Without oxygen, burning could not take place. Matches would not light. The fires that we use for cooking and heating could not burn, whether they were from coal or oil or gas or wood. The gasoline in the car and school bus would not burn, so cars and buses could not run.

Then, too, oxygen is one of the most important "building blocks" in the world. Oxygen combines with many different substances to build many different compounds. When substances burn, oxygen combines with carbon and makes carbon dioxide. Oxygen combines with hydrogen to make water. Oxygen combines with iron to make iron oxide. Oxygen combines with hydrogen to make compounds such as hydrogen peroxide. Oxygen combines with thousands of different substances to build useful compounds.

No doubt about it, oxygen is important. And there is a lot of this important substance on Earth. There is oxygen in the air. There is oxygen in the waters of the Earth. There is oxygen in the rocks and the soil of the Earth. This sandstone, for example, is mainly silicon and oxygen. ■

Of course there is another important use of oxygen to mention. All living things use oxygen in one way or another. *You* use oxygen. When you breathe in, you take in air. When you breathe out, you do not send out the same kind of air you took in. Of course, air you breathe out has more moisture in it than air you breathe in. But there is something else.

You inhale air with oxygen in it. In place of some of the oxygen you inhale, you breathe out a different gas, carbon dioxide. You do this with every breath. The air you exhale has more carbon dioxide in it than the air you inhale. The simple test in the investigation on the next page will show you. `INVESTIGATE`

AN INVESTIGATION into the Air You Breathe

Needed: a bicycle pump, two rubber balloons, two pieces of string, two glasses full of limewater

Fill one balloon with ordinary air, using the bicycle pump. ■ Tie the balloon with a string. Fill the other balloon with air from your lungs. ● Tie this balloon with a string.

Now let the air slowly and gently out of one balloon into the limewater in one glass.   Do the same with the other balloon and the other glass.

Here is what happened. ▲ ◆

Limewater turns a milky color when it meets carbon dioxide. Which air turned the limewater milky? Why?

Additional Investigation: Invent another way to do the limewater test of the air you breathe.

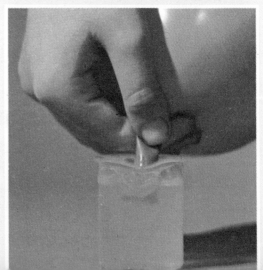

What You Do with Oxygen

As a candle burns, it takes oxygen from the air. The wax of the candle contains the element carbon. As the candle burns, it takes this carbon and combines it with oxygen. It gets the oxygen from the air. ■

As the candle combines carbon and oxygen, it produces light energy and heat energy. Perhaps you have already guessed what the candle combines carbon and oxygen into. The candle combines carbon and oxygen into carbon dioxide.

carbon + oxygen ⟶
        carbon dioxide + energy

The energy is heat and light energy.

A burning candle takes oxygen from the air and gives off carbon dioxide. *You* take oxygen from the air and give off carbon dioxide. A burning candle makes carbon dioxide by combining carbon and oxygen. *You* make carbon dioxide by combining carbon and oxygen in your body. Where do you get the carbon? From the food you eat. Sugar, bread, meat, and milk, all have carbon in them. Where do you get the oxygen? You breathe it in, of course.

A burning candle gives off energy. Do *you* produce energy? Put your hand on your mouth. Breathe out. Your breath is warm. The heat which

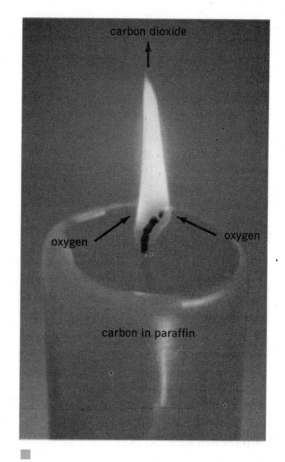

carbon dioxide

oxygen   oxygen

carbon in paraffin

■

made your breath warm is produced in your body.

In a burning candle,

carbon + oxygen ⟶
        carbon dioxide + energy

In your body,

carbon + oxygen ⟶
        carbon dioxide + energy

Does this mean, then, that burning is taking place in your body? No, not in the usual sense of burning with a flame. Heat, but no light, is given off by the **chemical reaction** in your body. Whenever a compound is broken down into other substances, or new compounds are built up, we say a chemical reaction has taken place. You will meet many such reactions.

Carbon and oxygen are combining now in your body, as you read this. Energy is being produced. However, this is not the only way you produce energy. There are many other chemical reactions in your body that give you energy. You will learn more about some of them later.

BEFORE YOU GO ON Study these statements and choose the correct responses. Your study will help fix in your mind the main concept of this section.

1. A burning candle uses up
   a. carbon dioxide   b. oxygen

2. Compared with the air we breathe in, the air we breathe out has
   a. less carbon dioxide   b. more carbon dioxide

3. Carbon and oxygen are combining now in your body to produce
   a. heat energy   b. light energy

USING WHAT YOU KNOW In a candle, and in our bodies,

carbon + oxygen ⟶ carbon dioxide + energy

What happens to the energy from a candle? What happens to the energy from our bodies?

ON YOUR OWN Probably compounds with carbon in them are burned every day in your home. Where are they burned? When are they burned?

7. The Return of Oxygen

We are using up the oxygen in the air. Oxygen is being used up every time we take a breath. Oxygen is being used up every time every animal takes a breath. Every time every fish passes water through its gills, oxygen is being used up.

Every time a lump of coal or a piece of wood is burned, oxygen in the air is used up. Whenever oil or gas is burned, oxygen is used up. Every automobile engine is using up oxygen as it burns gasoline.

Oxygen is combining with other elements, too. For example, rusting is using up oxygen.

Oxygen in the air is being used up all the time. It seems that it should have been all used up long ago! Yet there still is plenty of oxygen in the air.

It must be that oxygen is being put back into the air somehow. But how is it being put back?

A Green Plant in a Jar

In the year 1774 an English scientist named Priestley (PREEST·lee) put some green plants under glass jars. ■ Nothing could get in or out of the jars. Priestley found that the green plants grew inside the glass jars when

■

they had light. They did not grow if they did not have light. In the dark the plants soon died.

Priestley decided to try the same sort of investigation with an animal. Could an animal live in a closed glass jar, like a green plant? He put a mouse in a jar. Nothing could get in or out. He soon found that the mouse could live only a little while in the closed jar. After a while the mouse began to get sleepy. Soon it went to sleep. If it was left too long in the jar, the mouse died.

Priestley found a strange thing though. He found that if he put a green plant in the jar with the sleepy mouse, the mouse soon began to move about. The mouse became lively again!

By doing these investigations and other investigations as well, Priestley concluded that green plants give something to the air around them.

He also found that green plants do this in the light, but not in the dark.

What could a green plant give to the air that would make a sleepy mouse lively again? You might make up a hypothesis. Then try the investigation on the opposite page to get some evidence. **INVESTIGATE**

The Gas a Green Plant Makes

The green water plant called *Elodea* (ih·LOH·dee·ah) gives off bubbles when light is shining on it. When elodea plants are in the dark, the bubbles slow down and stop. ■

There is gas inside the bubbles, so this green plant is giving off a gas. We are able to see the gas being given off because the plant is under water. This green plant gives off a gas only when light is shining on it.

What is the gas that the elodea plant gives off in light? Here is a way of collecting the gas, so that it can be tested. ■ It is difficult, however, to collect pure oxygen. But when the gas is collected and tested, it turns out to be mostly *oxygen*. The plant gives off oxygen when light is falling on it.

Scientists have done many experiments which show that when light is falling on this green plant, *Elodea,* the plant gives off oxygen. Many other investigations and experiments by scientists have shown that all green plants do the same thing. *All green plants give oxygen to the air, when in the light*. The green plants use the energy of light to do this.

Now the mystery of the sleepy mouse that became lively again can be explained.

In the jar by itself, the mouse soon used up the oxygen in the jar. The mouse became sleepy. It needed oxygen. When a green plant was put in the jar, the mouse became lively again. The green plant gave off oxygen and the mouse used it.

AN INVESTIGATION into a Plant Under Water

Needed: an aquarium with healthy elodea plants and fish, a cardboard

Aquarium plants and fish are healthy if they are growing well. Place the aquarium in sunlight. ■ Observe the plants. From time to time you may see something like this. ●

Watch the bubbles rising. Then shut off the sunlight from the elodea plants with the cardboard. ▲

What happens to the bubbles when light is cut off? What do you observe? ◆

Additional Investigation: Instead of cardboard, use red cellophane or plastic. What happens to the bubbles? How do you explain your result?

Try other colors of cellophane or plastic. Also try the colorless kind. What do you observe in each case? How do you explain your observations?

●

▲

■

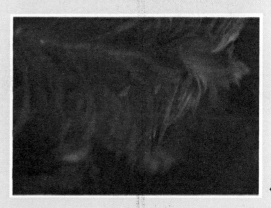

◆

125

carbon dioxide

oxygen

Another Cycle

It might seem that we have reached the end of this story. We have found out where the oxygen we use comes from. The story is not over, however. In a way, it never ends. Let us see why this is so.

If there is a green plant in view, take a good look at it. You and that green plant are partners in living. You need oxygen. The green plant gives off oxygen. You give off carbon dioxide. *The green plant takes in carbon dioxide.*

Whatever is burning now is using up oxygen, and it is also making carbon dioxide. Green plants are taking that carbon dioxide and making oxygen, which they put back into the air.

All this can be summed up neatly in a diagram. ■ Do you recognize this? It is a cycle. This one is called the **oxygen cycle**. The oxygen cycle is another cycle that is a part of your life.

Now the mystery of where *our* oxygen comes from can be explained. Although we are taking oxygen from the air, green plants are putting oxygen back into the air. They do not do this all the time, however. They do it only while light is shining on them.

Where does this light come from? It comes from the Sun, 93 million miles away. We depend on something 93 million miles away for the oxygen we breathe.

BEFORE YOU GO ON Study these statements and choose the correct responses. Your study will help fix in your mind the main concept of this section.

1. Every time we breathe in, we use up
   a. oxygen   b. carbon dioxide

2. Oxygen is put back into the air by
   a. green plants   b. animals

3. When giving off oxygen, a green plant uses up
   a. oxygen   b. carbon dioxide

4. A green plant can use energy from
   a. coal   b. the Sun

5. All green plants give off oxygen to the air
   a. in the light   b. all the time

USING WHAT YOU KNOW A cow in a green field uses the grass for food. What else does the grass give to the cow? What does the cow give to the grass?

8. The Main Concept: An Important Cycle

A crab crawling at the bottom of the sea is under an ocean of water. *You* are moving at the bottom of the atmosphere, under an ocean of air. The crab must take in water to live. You must take in air to live.

What is this important stuff you must breathe? Air is a mixture of different gases. It is made up of molecules of different substances.

Some of these molecules in air are elements—that is, they are molecules made up of one kind of atom. Oxygen is an element in the air. Some of the molecules in the air are compounds made up of different atoms. Carbon dioxide is a compound in the air. Air is a mixture of elements and compounds.

We know that one element in air is very important to us. It is oxygen. The oxygen in the air we breathe is used in our bodies. In our bodies the food we eat is combined with the oxygen we breathe. The result is energy, energy that makes us alive. Food is not enough. Our bodies cannot use food without oxygen.

Oxygen is important in other ways as well. Fuels such as coal and gasoline and oil and gas cannot burn without oxygen. When oxygen combines with carbon, the result is energy.

We use oxygen. Burning fuels use oxygen. Living things use oxygen. Living things combine oxygen with carbon and get energy for living.

One thing is very clear about this important substance. Oxygen is being used at a great rate.

All the oxygen ought to have been used up long ago.

There Is a Cycle

The oxygen in the air is being used in many ways. Yet the oxygen in the air has not been used up. Oxygen is still in the air because it is being put back by green plants. Green plants give off oxygen when they are in light. We depend on green plants not only for food but also for this important substance, oxygen.

What does a green plant use when giving off oxygen? Carbon dioxide. Where does the carbon dioxide come from? We and other living things give off carbon dioxide. When we combine oxygen and carbon in our bodies for energy, we make carbon dioxide and then breathe it out. Animals take in oxygen and give off carbon dioxide. In the foodmaking process green plants take in carbon dioxide and give off oxygen. ■ There is a cycle, then. Because there is a cycle, oxygen is not used up. The oxygen molecules you are breathing in right now, you will combine with other molecules into carbon dioxide molecules and breathe out. Some green plant will take in those carbon dioxide molecules you made. Then that green plant will give off oxygen molecules to the air. Those oxygen molecules may be used again. And again. And again.

The oxygen in the air is not used up because there is a cycle. You and every other living thing are a part of the oxygen cycle.

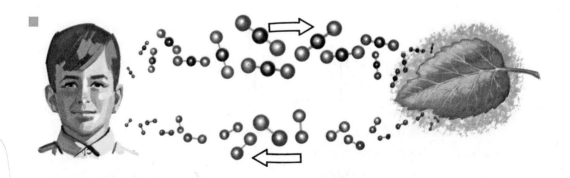

Fixing the Main Concepts

Study the statements below and choose the correct responses. Your study will help fix in your mind the main concepts of this unit.

1. Balloon B has more of one gas than balloon A. That
gas is

    a. oxygen   b. carbon dioxide

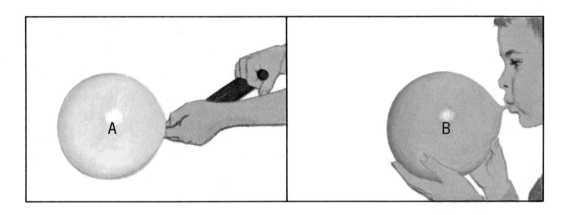

2. Balloon A has more of one gas than balloon B. That
gas is

    a. oxygen   b. carbon dioxide

3. If balloon A were emptied into limewater, the limewater would

    a. remain clear   b. become milky

4. If balloon B were emptied into limewater, the limewater would

    a. remain clear   b. become milky

5. Balloon A, compared with balloon B, has more of
the element

    a. oxygen   b. carbon dioxide

6. Balloon B, compared with balloon A, has more of the compound

     a. oxygen   b. carbon dioxide

7. If a green plant could be put into balloon B with light, the plant would soon use up most of the

     a. carbon dioxide   b. oxygen

8. An animal like a mouse would live longer in

     a. balloon A   b. balloon B

9. A mouse in balloon A would soon use up the element

     a. oxygen   b. nitrogen

10. When different elements combine, they form

     a. compounds   b. atoms

FOR YOUR READING   *The Rise and Fall of the Seas—The Story of the Tides,* by Ruth Brindze, published by Harcourt, Brace & World, 1964. How the Sun and the Moon draw up the oceans to make tides, how tides are measured and predicted, how men have made use of tides, and many other interesting things about the great waters on the Earth.

GOING FURTHER   In the investigation on page 125, the green plant elodea gave off bubbles in light. In the dark the plant stopped giving off bubbles.

Suppose you were to cover the aquarium completely with red cellophane or red plastic. Would the plant still give off bubbles?

Would it give off more or fewer bubbles under yellow cellophane? green cellophane? blue? orange?

Plan an investigation to see under which kind of light the elodea plant produces the most gas bubbles.

A New View
of Matter

How many different kinds of matter are around you right now?

Some are gases, like the gases in the air you are breathing. Some are liquids, like the water you drink. Some are solids, like the paper of this book. What different kinds of matter there are!

Yet we know that all matter is alike in this: all matter, whatever kind it is, is made up of tiny particles.

The gases you breathe, the water you drink, the paper of this page—most of the matter around you is made up of the tiny particles we call molecules. A molecule is the smallest part of a substance that still has the properties of that substance. A molecule of oxygen, for instance, is the smallest part of oxygen that still has the properties of oxygen. A molecule of water is the smallest part of water that still has the properties of water. ∎

Yet the tiny particles we call molecules are made up of still smaller particles. Molecules are made up of particles that we call atoms. Some molecules are made up of atoms that are all the same kind. Some molecules are made up of different atoms.

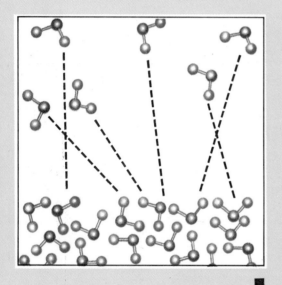

For instance, a molecule of oxygen is made up of two atoms bound tightly together. The atoms are alike. Since the two oxygen atoms are alike, oxygen is an element. An element is made up of only one kind of atom.

A molecule of water, however, is made up of different kinds of atoms. It has two atoms of hydrogen and one atom of oxygen, all tightly bound together. Water is a compound, for a compound is made up of atoms of different elements. The elements in a compound are not simply mixed together. They are tightly bound together by forces. They are chemically combined.

Particles and Changes

Matter is made up of particles, of arrangements of molecules and atoms. But these arrangements are not forever fixed and unchanging.

Put a drop of water on a plate, for example. Little by little the drop gets smaller, until it disappears. The drop of water evaporates, of course. The water changes from a liquid to a gas. The water molecules move away from the drop into the air. ■

As the water becomes a gas, the molecules are able to move around much more freely than they could in the liquid. Notice, however, that the molecules themselves have not changed. Each molecule is still made up of two atoms of hydrogen and one atom of oxygen. Each molecule is still a water molecule. Its atoms have not changed. The space between the molecules has changed: the molecules have moved around and taken a different position. This change from liquid to a gas is a physical change. Water that evaporates undergoes a physical change.

There is another important kind of change for particles. As you breathe in now, you are taking in molecules of oxygen. As you breathe out, you are sending out molecules of carbon dioxide. The molecules of oxygen that you breathe in are taken apart into atoms of oxygen in your body. Then these atoms of oxygen are combined with atoms of carbon (which you get from food) to make new molecules, molecules of carbon dioxide. So new molecules are formed out of the particles of the old ones.●

When atoms of oxygen and atoms of carbon combine to form molecules of carbon dioxide, this is a chemical change. Molecules can take part in a physical change or a chemical change. Matter can be changed because the particles of which matter is made up are in constant change.

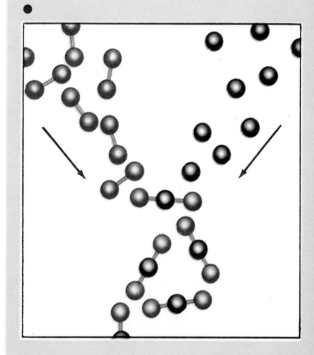

UNIT FIVE

THE FALL OF A TREE

The farmer was talking about his trees. "There was one tree I liked best of all," he said. "It was a huge oak. It must have been at least two hundred years old. A hawk liked to perch high on a top branch, to look around. That oak towered above the other trees.

"Then, one day, there was a big storm. The tree was weak. Its roots had been rotting slowly over the years. When the big storm came, the tree fell and lay there in the woods.

"Now, some people might have thought that that tree's work was done. But it wasn't. A green snake raised its family under that tree trunk. So did some chipmunks. In fact, quite a lot of living things made their homes in it. Ferns and mosses grew around it and on it. That tree began to become part of the woods again."

How can a dead tree become part of the woods again? Let us explore life in the woods, and the life of a tree.

AN INVESTIGATION into Where Green Plants Will Grow

Needed: fifteen or twenty zinnia, or bean, or radish, or squash seeds; eleven paper cups, two saucers, cotton, a little vinegar, soil, sand

First find out which seeds will grow. Soak all the seeds in water overnight. Then place them on wet cotton in a saucer. ■ Cover them with the other saucer. When a root begins to poke out of a seed, you will know that the seed is growing.●

Number eight of the paper cups, from 1 to 8. Plant one growing seed in each cup, under the different condi-

tions described on the opposite page. Put each seed about one-half inch below the surface of the soil.

Below are the results of one trial.▲ Under what conditions did the plants grow best? How do you know? Under what conditions was the growth poorest? How do you know?

Additional Investigation: Try planting seeds under still other conditions. Plant one growing seed in cups 9, 10, and 11 under different conditions that you think up. Which plant grows best? How do you explain your result?

Cup number	Growing conditions till the seedling grows 2 inches	How it grew
1	In good soil, in good light, and watered every day.	
2	In good soil, in good light, and watered every other day.	
3	In good soil, in good light, and watered every fifth day.	
4	In good soil, in a dark closet, and watered every other day.	
5	In good soil, in shade, and watered every day.	
6	In good soil, in good light, watered every day —but with a teaspoonful of vinegar added to the soil.	
7	In sand, in good light, and watered every day.	
8	In good soil, in good light, but with cup standing in a pot of water. Make small holes in bottom of the cup with a pencil point, to let water in.	
9	Do this one your way.	
10	Do this one your way.	
11	Do this one your way.	

1. We Grow a Plant

Most people think it is easy to grow a tree. After all, all you have to do is get the seed of a tree and plant it. The seed grows, and in time you have a tree.

Is it easy for a seed to grow? Find out by trying the investigation on these two pages. INVESTIGATE

Where Will a Green Plant Grow?

Some of the seeds in the investigation did not grow. A seed will not grow just anywhere. Many, many investigations and experiments have proved it. A seed has to have certain conditions around it to grow. That is, a seed has to have a certain **environment** (en·vy·ron·ment). No two seeds had the same growing conditions. The kind of soil, the number of times the seeds were watered, and the amount of light were all part of the environment of each seed. You may have thought of another condition, too.

The eleven seeds in the investigation were in eleven different environments, then. You probably had little trouble deciding which environment was bad and which was good for the growth of the seeds.

Now look at these plants. ■ What do you think is lacking in their environments? Water is lacking.

Plants grow best in the right environment, that is clear. But there is more to it than that. There are many different kinds of plants. Different kinds of plants need different environments. The best environment for one kind of plant can be a poor environment for another kind of plant. An environment in which a water plant can grow well is not good for a land plant. The desert is the right environment for this cactus plant. ● The desert is not the right environment for a maple tree or for a jack-in-the-pulpit. ▲

Most green plants living on land must have soil, water, light, and heat as part of their environment. But that is not enough. A plant must have the *right kind* of soil. Some plants, such as sugar beets, grow well in sandy soil where other plants cannot grow.

A plant must have the right amount of light. Some plants grow

■

well in the sunlight; some, such as violets, grow well in shade. A plant must have the right amount of water. If too much water reaches a plant, the plant may actually drown. If there is too little water, a plant may not grow properly.

There are other things too that a plant must have, as you will see later on. But we can say all this in a single sentence. A plant must have the right environment to grow.

It isn't so easy to grow a tree after all, is it?

BEFORE YOU GO ON Study these statements and choose the correct responses. Your study will help fix in your mind the main concept.

1. Plants
   a. can grow without water
   b. must have water to grow

2. Plants grow best in
   a. the right environment
   b. any environment

USING WHAT
YOU KNOW
1. A cactus plant and a maple tree are both green plants. Both need soil, water, light, and heat in their environments. However, a cactus cannot live where a maple lives. How do their environments differ?

2. What do *you* have to have in *your* environment?

ON YOUR OWN
A boy planted ten bean seeds in good soil, putting each seed one inch below the surface. Each seed got the same amount of water and sunlight. Seven of the ten seeds poked their way through the soil. Three seeds did not. What went wrong?

2. The Scientist and the Willow Tree

In the year 1605 a Belgian scientist named Jan van Helmont took a willow branch and planted it. He did not plant it in the ground, however. He planted the branch in a tub of soil, with a lid on it. ■ For the next 5 years, Jan van Helmont watered that willow carefully.

What was he looking for? He wanted to know where the willow was getting the food substances that made it grow. The willow kept getting bigger. It had to be getting these substances from somewhere. Where was it getting them?

In a way this was a foolish question. Most people thought they knew the answer already. The answer was that the willow plant took substances *from the soil* to grow. Of course, every one had known that for a thousand years!

However, van Helmont was a scientist. He wanted evidence. So he set up an investigation. Suppose the willow did take substances from the soil as it grew. Then, as the willow grew and weighed more, the soil ought to weigh less.

Van Helmont weighed the willow branch before planting it. It weighed 5 pounds. He weighed the dry soil. It weighed 200 pounds. Then he planted the branch and watered it with rainwater for 5 years.

At the end of 5 years, the willow branch had become a willow tree, and it weighed 169 pounds. ● It had gained 164 pounds in weight. If people were right, the willow had taken 164 pounds of substances from the soil in the tub. Van Helmont took the willow tree out of the tub. Then he dried the soil in the tub and weighed it.

The soil weighed almost the same as it had when he first put the willow in it. It had lost only 3 ounces in weight!

This was an astonishing result. Where *did* the willow get the substances for its growth, then? Van Helmont thought of an answer, based on his experiment. What answer would you make? After you have thought it over, check your answer against van Helmont's, at the bottom of the next page.

Jan van Helmont was right, so far as he went. However, there was more to learn. Today, more than 350 years later, we know more about

141

that willow tree—after many investigations. Are there substances in soil that a plant might take? Try the investigation on the opposite page for yourself. INVESTIGATE

There Are Substances in Soil

As the investigation shows, there are substances in soil. Do plants use these substances? Yes. Water dissolves these substances. Then green plants like the willow take up the

---

Jan van Helmont concluded that the willow must have gotten its substances from the rainwater he gave it.

water, and the substances in it, through their roots.

These plants are growing in a field rich in the substances plants take from the soil. ■ This plant is growing in a field poor in those substances. ● Is this plant as tall as the others? Why?

Green plants take from soil two kinds of substances. One kind is called **nitrates** (NY·trayts). These are compounds of nitrogen and oxygen. The other kind is called **phosphates** (FOS-fayts), compounds of phosphorus and oxygen. The corn plants in the second field will need an amount of nitrates for good growth. ● And they will need

Potash

AN INVESTIGATION into Some Substances in Soil

Needed: a jar of garden soil, half a jar of distilled water, a wad of cotton, a funnel, a beaker

Distilled water is pure water: it has no substances dissolved in it. (You can obtain distilled water from a pharmacy.) Pour the distilled water into the garden soil and shake it. Let the mixture of soil and water stand overnight. If there are substances in the soil that can dissolve in the water, this will give them time to do so.

Pack cotton into the funnel. This makes a filter. Pour the water from the jar through this filter, to strain out the soil. ■ Only the water, and any substances dissolved in it, go through the cotton filter into the beaker.

Now evaporate the water in the beaker by letting it stand in a warm place or by heating the water gently on a hot plate.

Here are the results of one trial. Is anything left in the beaker? Where did it come from? ●

Did the soil contain substances that could dissolve in water?

Additional Investigation: How could you show that the distilled water you used in the investigation above has no dissolved substance in it?

There are substances in the soil that plants use. Then why didn't Jan van Helmont find that the soil in which his willow grew lost a lot of weight? The answer is that the willow used only a very small amount of these substances, compared to the weight of the soil. Out of 200 pounds of soil, the willow used only about 3 ounces of substances in 5 years.

From Soil, Water, and Air

In 5 years that willow gained 164 pounds of substances. It got only a very little of them from the soil in the tub. Where did it get all the rest? Was van Helmont right? Did the plant get the rest from the water?

Jan van Helmont was partly right. The willow did get substances that were dissolved in the water. The willow also used the water. That was not the whole answer, however, for the willow got substances from another place as well. Today, after many investigations, after the work of many men, we know more about the substances green plants use.

A green plant uses substances that it takes from the air. It takes from the air a gas that has no color and no odor, called carbon dioxide. *A green plant can take carbon dioxide*

a quantity of phosphates at the same time. However, wheat plants need different amounts of nitrates and phosphates than do corn plants. Different kinds of plants may use different amounts of these and other substances in the soil.

Green plants take substances from the soil as they grow. These substances must be put back into the soil. If they are not, what you see in the second picture on page 142 happens. **Fertilizers** are substances that we add to soil to make up for the substances taken from it by plants. This fertilizer contains mainly nitrates and phosphates. ■

and water and use these to make other substances like sugars, starches, and wood fibers.

This is one of the most important discoveries ever made by scientists. Van Helmont's willow made most of the substances in it out of carbon dioxide and water.

Green plants can make foods such as sugars and starches from carbon dioxide and water. However, green plants can do this only under certain conditions.

You probably know some of these conditions. Will a green plant grow if the weather is very cold? No. A green plant needs heat. Will a green plant grow in the dark? No. A green plant needs light.

With heat and light, a green plant can make food from substances dissolved in water and from carbon dioxide in the air. Colorless plants, such as mushrooms, cannot do what green plants do. They cannot make their own food.

Where does a green plant get these substances? From the Earth, of course. The Earth (and the air around it) is the great storehouse of soil and water and air for green plants. Where does a green plant get heat and light, though? The heat and light that green plants need travel 93 million miles through space—from the Sun.

Green plants use both the Earth and the Sun.

BEFORE YOU GO ON Study these statements and choose the correct responses. Your study will help fix in your mind the main concept of this section.

1. To make sugars, green plants need the substances water and
    a. carbon dioxide   b. light

2. To make sugars, green plants also need
    a. cold   b. light

3. For a plant to use the substances in soil, they must be
    a. dissolved   b. solid

1. Van Helmont was a scientist. Because he was a scientist, what did he do?

2. What evidence shows that there are dissolved substances in soil water?

3. Which of these statements is accurate? Why?
   a. Green plants can make sugars from carbon dioxide and water.
   b. All plants can make sugars from carbon dioxide and water.

You know more now about how plants grow than van Helmont did. Why is this so?

3. An Apple Tree Is a Factory

You know what this is, of course. ■ Did you know that apart from the water in it, it is made mainly of sugar?

An apple has a good deal of sugar in it. That is one of the several reasons we like to eat it.

Yet an apple tree does not take in sugar. An apple tree takes in substances from the soil water and from the air. None of these substances is sugar. Yet an apple has sugar in it. Somehow, an apple tree makes sugar.

Isn't this remarkable, when you think of it? You certainly could not tell by looking at an apple tree that it is doing such a thing. Let us find out what is going on here. A good place to begin is with this question: What is sugar made of? The investigation on the opposite page will help you find out. INVESTIGATE

AN INVESTIGATION into What Sugar Is Made Of

Needed: sugar, a test tube holder, a Pyrex test tube, an alcohol lamp or a Bunsen burner

Make sure that the Pyrex test tube is dry. Then place about a quarter of an inch of sugar in it. Put the tube in the test tube holder.

Heat the sugar gently, holding the tube as shown.■ *Remember that a tube being heated should never be pointed toward anyone!* Be sure to move the tube around so that every part of the sugar is heated equally. As the sugar gets darker, some vapor will be given off. Heat the tube until the sugar is black. Here is what happened in one trial.●

What do you observe on the side of the tube? What is it?

What is the black substance at the bottom of the tube?

Additional Investigation: Sugar and starch are made of the same substances, but the amounts are different. Show that at least one substance found in sugar is also found in starch.

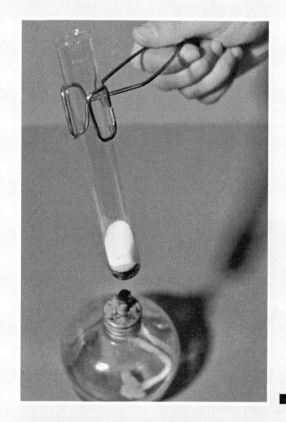

■

●

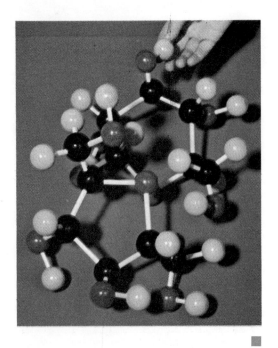

A molecule of sucrose is made up of 12 atoms of carbon, 22 atoms of hydrogen, and 11 atoms of oxygen. A model of a molecule of sucrose looks like this. ■

There is a shorter way of saying what is in a molecule of sucrose. A chemist simply writes $C_{12}H_{22}O_{11}$. **C** stands for carbon, **H** stands for hydrogen, and **O** for oxygen. The numbers stand for the number of atoms of each in the sucrose molecule. (Instead of asking for the sucrose, you could say, "Please pass the C twelve H twenty-two O eleven.") $C_{12}H_{22}O_{11}$ is the formula for sucrose.

Another kind of sugar is called *glucose* (GLUE·kohs). An apple makes glucose. The formula for glucose is $C_6H_{12}O_6$. Can you tell from this formula how many atoms of carbon, hydrogen, and oxygen there are in glucose? You can check your answer by counting atoms in this model of a glucose molecule. ●

What Sugar Is Made Of

When sugar is heated enough, a black substance appears. This black substance is carbon. There is carbon in sugar.

What about the drops that appear when sugar is heated? They are drops of water. Water, you know, is made up of hydrogen and oxygen. So there are hydrogen and oxygen in sugar, as well as carbon.

There are different kinds of sugar, but they are all made up of atoms of carbon, hydrogen, and oxygen. The table sugar used in the investigation is a kind of sugar called *sucrose* (SUE·krohs). (Try saying "Please pass the sucrose" next time.)

The Food Factory

Most green plants make the kind of sugar called glucose, to begin with. Then, having made glucose, the plants change it into other kinds of sugar. For instance, a sugar cane plant first makes glucose. Then it changes the glucose into sucrose, from which table sugar comes. Fruits like apples and oranges are storage places of sugar.

In many plants the sugar is changed to *starch*. Some plants store the starch. Plants such as the cactus and rhubarb store starch in their stems. A potato is made of starch stored in the underground stem of the potato plant. Sugars and starches are **carbohydrates,** compounds of carbon, hydrogen, and oxygen.

The sugars that plants make can be changed in other ways, too. Sugars can be changed into **fats.** Fats are made up of carbon, hydrogen, and oxygen atoms, as sugars are. But the number of atoms and the way they are combined is different. The green plant shifts the atoms around to make fats out of sugars.

Plants can add other substances to the sugars they make. A plant may start with sugar, for instance, to make a substance we call **protein.** To make protein, atoms of nitrogen are combined with carbon, hydrogen, and oxygen. Like sugars and starches and fats, protein is also an important substance.

Why are sugars and starches and fats and proteins important? Perhaps you already know the answer. Sugars, starches, fats, and proteins are *foods.* You do not have to be told how important foods are. Remember that foods are not only necessary to you. Foods are necessary to every living thing.

The green plant is a kind of food factory, in a way. The green plant makes sugars, starches, fats, and proteins. The green plant is also a storage place for these foods that animals must eat.

The green plant must have energy to make sugars, starches, fats, and proteins. Where does the energy come from? Try the investigation on the next page to find out. INVESTIGATE

AN INVESTIGATION into Energy for a Green Plant

Needed: twelve radish seeds, three small jars, blotting paper

Line the jars with blotting paper. Label the jars 1, 2, and 3. Put four radish seeds around the side of each jar, between the glass and the blotting paper. Wet the blotting paper. ■

Put jar 1 in a dark closet or drawer where it can get no light. ● Put jar 2 where it will get light only from an electric lamp. ▲ Put jar 3 where it will get some sunlight from time to time. ◆ Do not forget to keep the blotters damp.

Observe how the seeds grow. Is light necessary? Is sunlight necessary? Here is what happened in one trial. ★

Additional Investigation: Does a red lamp make a difference?

Study these statements and choose the correct responses. Your study will help fix in your mind the main concept of this section.

1. Glucose, sucrose, and starch are made up of carbon, hydrogen, and
   a. nitrogen   b. oxygen

2. Proteins are different from starches because they contain
   a. nitrogen   b. oxygen

3. Fats are made up of carbon, hydrogen, and
   a. nitrogen   b. oxygen

1. Glucose sugar and sucrose sugar are made up of the same kinds of atoms. What is the difference between glucose and sucrose, then?

2. A potato has starch in it. From what substance was the starch made?

3. Which of these statements is more accurate?
   a. Green plants make food for the world.
   b. Animals make food for the world.

Is the model of a molecule of glucose, on page 149, what a glucose molecule really looks like?

4. A Tree Grows

Suppose that about half an inch of a small nail was hammered into a tree such as a willow or a red maple. (It would not harm the tree.) Suppose that the nail was driven into the tree just 4 feet above the ground. ■ And suppose that the tree grew about 1 foot taller every year.

How high above the ground do you think the nail would be in 5 years' time?

You can see the answer in this picture. ● Is it what you expected? After all, the tree grew taller. Then why is the nail where it is?

The investigation on the opposite page will help you to answer this question. Try it. INVESTIGATE

Inside a Tree

The marks on the sunflower plant, in the investigation, showed that the plant grew taller at the tip, not at the bottom. This is how a plant or a tree gets taller. It grows at the tip. Can you see why the nail driven into the tree did not rise, although the tree became taller?

A tree grows taller at the top, just as a sunflower does. There is a reason for this. Let us look at how a tree is made.

AN INVESTIGATION into Growth in a Plant

Needed: Sunflower seeds, flower pots, soil, a marking pen, a ruler

Plant some sunflower seeds in the pots. (Follow the directions on the seed package.) When the young plants are about two inches high, make a black dot on the stem with the marking pen, about an inch above the soil. ■

What do you think will happen to the height of this mark as the young plants grow? As the plant gets taller, measure the height of the mark above the soil.

Here is what happened in one trial.●

Additional Investigation: As a plant grows, add more marks to its stem, one inch apart. Does growth take place evenly all along a stem? Or does the stem grow more in one place?

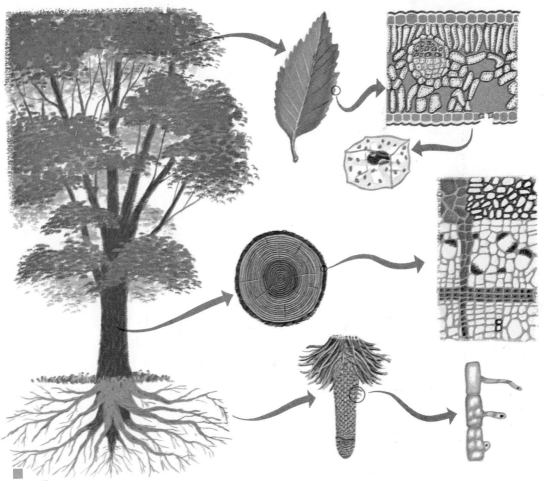

To see how a tree is made, look at little thin slices of it under a microscope. The slices of tree are made up of tiny boxlike structures. ■ These tiny structures are **cells.** As you examine different parts of a tree under the microscope, you will see that the cells are not all alike. Different parts of a tree are made up of different kinds of cells.

The same thing is true of a plant, a sunflower, for instance. Plants, like trees, are made up of different kinds of cells. How large are these cells? Fifty of the cells at the tip of a sunflower would fit into the period at the end of this sentence. A cell is the smallest living part of any living thing. You need to look at cells through a microscope to see them.

A tree or a plant grows longer mainly at its top. Let us look at the cells at the top, then, and see what happens there.

A Cell Grows

Suppose that we could observe one cell at the tip of a growing plant, watching it through a microscope to see if anything happens. While we watch, we see a strange thing. The cell becomes two cells.

The tip of the plant is growing. It grows by **cell division**. That is, each cell at the tip divides into two cells. In a little while each of the

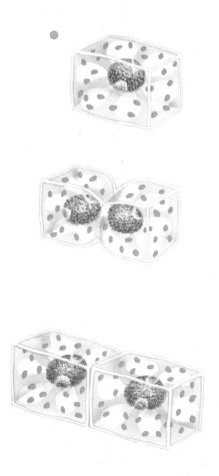

two new cells will divide. There will be four cells where there was only one to begin with. In time, each of the four new cells will divide. (How many new cells will this make at the tip of the plant?) In a short time, the new cells grow and become as large as the cells that divided. As this happens, the tip of the plant is getting longer and longer, growing.

Notice that as the cell divides what is inside it divides as well. For this reason, the growing cells at the tip of the plant are very much alike.

When a plant is growing, the cells at the tips of its branches are dividing. These cells at the tip of the branches are alike. If you have pulled up a small plant and a larger plant like it, you know that roots grow, too. When a plant is growing, the cells at the tip of its roots are dividing. These root tip cells are alike. A plant grows taller by cell division. Its roots grow longer by cell division, and reach deeper into the soil.

The nail in the tree did not change its height above the ground as the tree grew taller. Did you observe something about the nail that *did* change? If you did not, turn back to page 152 and take another look at the pictures.

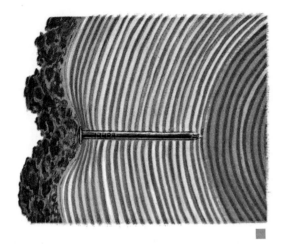

The nail seems to have gone far-ther into the tree. This is not what really happened, however. What happened is that the tree has grown out around the nail. In a few years more the nail may disappear. The tree may grow over it. ■

Since this is so, what must the layer of cells shown in green be doing?

BEFORE YOU GO ON
Study these statements and choose the correct responses. Your study will help fix in your mind the main concept of this section.

1. A tree grows in height at the

    a. tip   b. middle

2. A tree grows in width because of the dividing cells in its

    a. trunk   b. tip

3. Into whichever part of a tree we look with a microscope, we find

    a. sugar   b. cells

USING WHAT YOU KNOW
1. Here are three different pictures of a cell dividing. They are not in the right order. What is the right order?

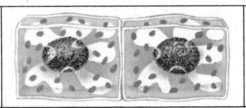

2. If you could look at a bit of a geranium plant under a microscope, what would you expect to see? Why?

ON YOUR OWN   Do you think that a plant can grow if its cells stop dividing? Why?

5. A Tree Falls

For many years a white oak tree grew and grew in a woods on a farm. It grew in a wet place, but white oaks like wet places. The white oak became a tall tree, 80 feet high. It became a good home for other living things, for animals and plants. It was a home for birds, for insects, for a family of raccoons. It gave shade to deer. It gave shade to many plants that must have shade to grow, such as ferns and mosses. Such plants cannot live in bright sunlight. ● The white oak received the bright light of the sun and sheltered the plants below. (Next time

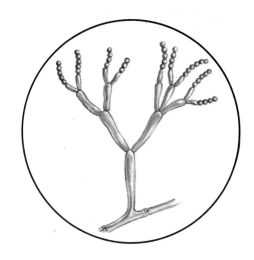

you go to a woods, examine the plants that grow in the shade. They are different from the plants growing in bright sunlight.)

In time, however, the oak tree fell. The farmer did not remove the fallen tree. He left it there as a shelter for the small animals he knew lived in his woods. Perhaps the oak tree would shelter some toads, or a green snake, or a garter snake. These animals eat their fill of insects that might harm crops. Farmers welcome such animals.

So the white oak tree lay in the woods. Have you ever thought what a woods might be like if all the trees remained where they fell? A woods would become clogged with dead trees, in time. Yet this does not happen. Dead trees disappear.

How does a dead tree disappear? Not because farmers take the trees away. The investigation on the opposite page will give you a good clue to the answer. INVESTIGATE

A Tree Starts to Disappear

A tree is made of cells. Even when the tree is dead, these cells have food stored in them. It is not the kind of food that you eat, to be sure. But it is food for certain plants, called **fungi** (FUN·jy). The molds that grow on bread are fungi. There are other fungi besides molds, however. Here are some other fungi. ■ ●

Fungi are plants. However, there is an important difference between fungi and the green plants we know so well. Green plants make their own food. Fungi do not make their own

158

AN INVESTIGATION
into a Piece of Bread

Needed: a piece of stale bread, a jar with a cover, a magnifying glass

Place the piece of bread in the jar. Add 5 drops of water to the bread. Then cover the jar, and put it in a warm place —but not in sunlight. ■

Observe the bread every day. Here is what happened in one trial.● A growth has formed on the bread. It is a mold, living and growing on the stale bread. Use the magnifying glass to examine the mold.▲ The tiny black balls are called spore cases. Each spore case is full of **spores.** A spore is a living cell that can grow into a mold plant.

The bread is being eaten by the mold and by other growths that appear on it. What will happen to the bread in time?

Additional Investigation: Where did the mold come from? Design an investigation to find out.

 ■

 ●

 ▲

159

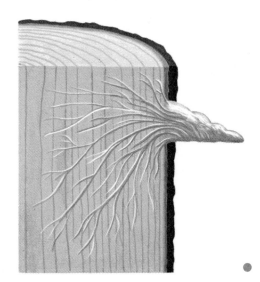

food. Green plants use **chlorophyll** (KLOR·uh·fil), a green substance in their cells, to make their food. Fungi have no chlorophyll in them. They cannot make their own food.

Where do these plants get food, then? They feed on other plants, or on food that is already made. Some fungi, such as bread mold, feed on bread, flour, and grain. Other fungi,

such as the blue molds, feed and grow on fruit. And still other fungi feed on wood in dead trees.

Have you ever seen fungi like these? ■ They are called bracket fungi. The body of the fungus (FUNG-gus) is made of threads reaching into the tree. The fungus threads travel deep into a dead tree and feed on the cells of the tree. ● The part growing out of the trunk, called the bracket, holds the spores. The spores can fall on other trees and give rise to more bracket fungi.

Fungi feed on the dead tree. Soon the tree begins to fall apart. It is starting to disappear, for it is being eaten by other plants. But that is not all that is happening.

A Tree Decays

Now the dead tree is overgrown with mosses. Even ferns are growing on it, their roots pushing down into the bark and below it. They too are helping to break up the tree. Fungi too are everywhere, on the tree and under the bark.

Lift up a piece of bark: insects scurry about. Slugs feed on the tree, hidden beneath the bark. Snails are there too. ▲

Push the tree and it gives way: it has little strength. Here, near the

♦

ground, it is crumbling almost into powder. This powder was once hard wood. ♦ Now the wood is breaking down. We say that the wood is **decaying** (dih·KAY·ing). This decaying wood is making the soil richer. As it decays, the wood becomes mixed with the soil. It becomes part of the soil. The wood becomes **humus** (HYOO-mus) in the soil. Humus is made up of bits of decayed plants and animals. Thus the tree is returning substances to the soil that it once took away from the soil.

It is plain to see that the dead white oak is now giving life to thousands of plants and animals. Yet there are billions upon billions of plants living in the tree that you cannot see, for they are too small. These

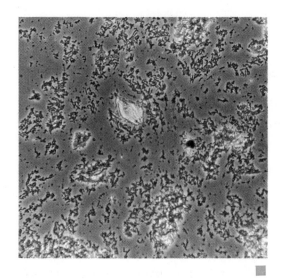

scope, some of the decay bacteria in soil look like this. ■ Small as they are, and simple as they look, they are living plants.

plants are the decay bacteria, tiny one-celled, colorless plants found in the soil. The decay bacteria are the main plants that feed on the tree and cause it to decay. You may remember that bacteria are not able to make their own food. Seen through a micro-

These bacteria that cause decay are very important to us. By breaking down dead plants and dead animals, bacteria make it possible for life to go on. The bacteria cause the tree to return substances to the soil. If substances were not returned to the soil, life could not go on. If plants took from the soil and never gave anything back, there would soon be nothing more to take.

The fungi and bacteria that cause decay are very important to us. If they did not return substances to the soil, green plants could not grow. We would have no food.

BEFORE YOU GO ON
Study these statements and choose the correct responses. Your study will help fix in your mind the main concept of this section.

1. Unlike a fungus, a green plant
   a. can make its own food
   b. cannot make its own food

2. Without bacteria, there would be no
   a. decay   b. soil

3. We expect to find chlorophyll in
   a. leaves   b. fungi

USING WHAT
YOU KNOW

1. What is one difference between a green plant and a fungus plant?

2. Why are decay bacteria important?

3. Which of these statements is accurate? Why?
   a. Decaying trees and plants make the soil richer.
   b. Decaying trees and plants make the soil poorer.

6. Three Seedlings

That white oak tree that fell and returned to the soil had a useful life. It made food and wood. It gave shelter to plants and animals. It gave food to insects and fungi. Yet it did still more. It made more of itself. The white oak tree made more white oak trees.

The white oak had the help of a squirrel, however. If you have ever watched a squirrel you know that he will carry an acorn far from a tree. As squirrels do, this squirrel buried some of the white oak's acorns. He buried some near the tree, and he buried others some distance away. And as squirrels do, he forgot some of them, and left them buried in the soil.

163

Some of those buried acorns sprouted. A young white oak seedling grew just about where the big tree had fallen, in the woods near the stream. The squirrel had buried another acorn across the road, up on the sunny hill. Another white oak seedling grew there, near a rock. Next to that white oak seedling there sprouted the seedling of a staghorn *sumac* (SUE·mak).

A scientist who has made a study of how plants grow could tell you something about the future of those three seedlings. He could tell you these things because he knows what kind of environment they need.

The white oak seedling in the woods near the stream would grow well.

The white oak seedling on the sunny hill would not grow as well as the one in the damp woods.

The staghorn sumac on the sunny hill would grow well enough.

How could a scientist know this? The answer has to do with the environment of each seedling. Environment, remember, means the conditions in which a plant or an animal lives. Let us see how important environment is.

The Importance of Environment

Here are three animals. ■ Can you think of an environment in which each one *cannot* live?

The bird cannot live under water. The fish cannot live on land. The frog cannot live in a desert. Each

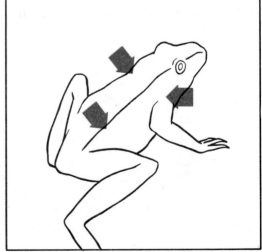

of these animals is so made that it can live in a certain environment. We say that each animal is **adapted** to a certain environment.

The bird is adapted to living in air. It has lungs. ● Lungs take oxygen from air. Lungs cannot take oxygen from water. Lungs adapt the bird to living in air.

A frog has lungs and breathes air. But it must also use its skin in breathing. The moist skin of a frog takes oxygen from the air. ▲ If a frog's skin dries, the frog will die. It will not get enough oxygen. So a frog's skin must remain moist. A frog is adapted to living where its skin remains moist. There are no frogs living in deserts.

The fish, however, is adapted to living in water. The fish has gills. ◆ Gills can take oxygen from water. The oxygen is dissolved in the water. Gills adapt the fish to living in water.

You can see why a bird cannot live under water, and why a fish cannot live on land. What about a frog? Why can't a frog live in a desert?

Each of these animals—frog, fish, bird—is adapted to a special environment. Indeed, this is true of every living thing. Each grows best in its special environment.

You may be wondering about man. Doesn't man live in many different places on this planet? Is there a

◆

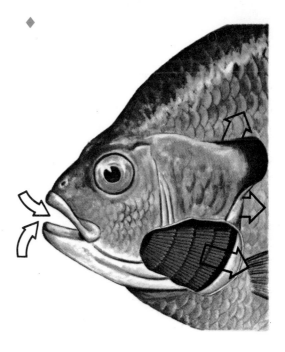

special environment for him, then? There is. Notice, for instance, that when man goes under water he takes air with him. ■ When he goes into space, he takes air and food and other things as well. There is an environment to which man is adapted.

Each living thing grows best in its special environment and grows poorly in other environments—if it grows at all. Environment can make the difference between growing and not growing, between life and death.

Now we know something of the importance of environment. Let us get back to our three seedlings. There is the white oak seedling in the forest near the stream. There is the white oak seedling on the sunny hill. And there is the staghorn sumac seedling on the hill. What about their environments?

An Environment for a White Oak Tree

A scientist who studies environments, and how living things are adapted to environments, is called an *ecologist* (eh·KOL·eh·jist). Ecologists know the best environment for a plant or an animal.

For example, suppose you told an ecologist that you had seen a fine weeping willow tree. He could tell you a good deal about the environment of the tree without ever having seen it. He could tell you, for instance, that the willow was growing where its roots had enough water. This is part of the environment that a willow tree must have in order to grow well.

An ecologist could describe the environment in which the white oak had grown. Ecologists have learned that a white oak tree lives best in an environment with soil that holds a fair amount of water. They have learned that staghorn sumac lives well enough in dry soil, but not in soil as dry as a desert. A cactus, however, can live in the dry deserts of the southwestern parts of the United States.

Do you see how an ecologist could predict the future of the white oak seedlings and of the staghorn sumac seedling, too? The ecologist knows that the white oak seedling in the moist soil near the stream is in the environment to which it is best adapted. That environment has been made even better by the decayed tree. The decayed tree has added humus to the soil. With more humus in it, the soil can hold more water. Moreover, the sun's light can reach the white oak seedling through the space where the old white oak once stood.

Up on the sunny hillside, the other white oak seedling receives plenty of sunlight, too. But its soil has little humus in it and is not so rich. Its soil cannot hold much water. The white oak seedling on the hill does not have its best environment. The staghorn sumac, however, is adapted to just this environment. It is adapted to rather dry soil. The sumac seedling can grow well enough here on the hill. The white oak seedling on the hill cannot grow well.

A living thing lives and grows best in the environment to which it is adapted. The better that environment, the better the living thing will grow. This is true for white oak trees, for birds, for frogs, for fish, for every plant and animal. It is true for you, too.

BEFORE
YOU GO ON
Study these statements and choose the correct responses. Your study will help fix in your mind the main concept of this section.

1. We say a living thing is adapted to an environment when it is
    a. fitted to live in the environment
    b. not fitted to live in the environment

2. A staghorn sumac is adapted to
    a. moist soil   b. dry soil

3. An ecologist is a scientist who studies
    a. the environment only
    b. living things and their environment

USING WHAT
YOU KNOW
1. Name three animals. For each animal, name an environment in which that animal cannot live.

2. How are *you* adapted for life on land?

ON YOUR OWN
Trees growing on city streets usually do not grow as well as trees growing in the woods. Why?

7. The Main Concept: A Living Thing in Its Environment

What would you expect to find in a pond like this one?■ You might expect to find fish, some water snails, perhaps some tadpoles. Certainly you would expect water plants.

You would be very much surprised to find a cow or a cactus plant living under water. You know that a living thing is adapted to a special environment. You expect certain living things, like a big tree, to live in a forest, not in a desert. You expect a whale to live in the sea, not in a forest.

All living things are adapted to their environment. This concept helps us in understanding the where and how of living things. Knowing this concept, we can understand the needs of a cactus, or a fish, or a sea gull. We can understand the life of a tree.

Because we know something of the environment of a tree, we can plant the seed where it will grow best. If we want a white oak, we plant the acorn in a wet place. If we want a staghorn sumac, we plant its seed in a dry place. If we want wheat, we prepare the field so that the wheat seeds will grow well.

Give a tree its proper environment and the tree will grow well. Its roots will take in water and the substances dissolved in water. Its leaves will take in carbon dioxide.

Using energy from the light of the sun, the green plant will make food. In its green leaves, carbon dioxide and water will combine to form sugar. Once sugar is formed, the green plant will combine it with nitrogen to form proteins, or it will change the sugar to form starches or fats.

We depend on green plants for our very life. All living things depend on green plants. Green plants are the food factories of the world.

Sooner or later a tree dies and falls. Yet this is not the end. Fungi and bacteria of decay now live on the tree. The tree becomes a good environment for other living things. Fungi, bacteria, insects, and small animals live in it—and on it. At last the tree crumbles. Its body adds humus to the soil. Other plants grow well in the enriched soil.

An acorn falls on the place where the tree stood. The soil is enriched by decayed wood. The acorn grows in the enriched soil. A seedling grows tall. Once again a living thing thrives because the environment fits it. And the living thing fits the environment.

Every living thing is adapted to its own environment.

Fixing the Main Concepts

TESTING YOURSELF   Study the statements below and choose the correct responses. Your study will help fix in your mind the main concepts of this unit.

1. To start growing, a seed needs
   a. water   b. light

2. To grow, a green plant needs
   a. light   b. darkness

3. A cactus and a fir tree need
   a. the same environment
   b. different environments

4. Plants make sugars from water and
   a. carbon dioxide   b. oxygen

5. Sugars can be made by
   a. all plants   b. green plants

6. To make proteins, a plant uses
   a. nitrogen   b. wood

7. A tree grows taller at
a. its top   b. its middle

8. When a tree is growing, its cells are
a. dividing   b. subtracting

9. As a tree decays, it is food mainly for
a. frogs and snakes   b. bacteria and fungi

10. A decaying tree adds humus and substances to the soil. This makes the environment
a. better for seedlings   b. worse for seedlings

FOR YOUR READING

1. *Discovering Plants*, by Glenn O. Blough, published by McGraw-Hill, New York, 1966. This book will help you investigate plants from the roots up.

2. *Because of a Tree*, by Lorus J. and Margery Milne, published by Atheneum Publishers, 1963. Here you will find out how different trees are important to other living things in their environment and, in turn, depend upon them.

3. *Maple Tree*, by Millicent E. Selsam, published by William Morrow and Company, 1968. This book's beautiful photographs help you follow the life cycle of a maple tree from seed to seed.

4. *Research Adventures for Young Scientists*, by George Barr, published by McGraw Hill, New York, 1964. One section of this book, called "Plant Investigations," will give you many ideas for your own investigations of plant life.

GOING FURTHER

An Investigation

Did you realize that yeast is a fungus? It is a colorless, microscopic plant. Yeast can grow well in a solution of sugar. As yeast grows, it gives off carbon dioxide gas. The faster yeast grows, the more carbon dioxide it gives off.

If you can observe the amount of carbon dioxide gas given off, you will know how well yeast is growing. The environment in which yeast grows best will result in the most gas.

To observe carbon dioxide gas, make a sucrose sugar solution by dissolving 4 level tablespoonfuls of sucrose in a quart of water.

Put some sugar solution in a small jar. Be sure that the jar is filled to the brim. Add a teaspoonful of powdered yeast to the solution. Cover the jar with a dish. ■ Place the jar in water upside down, without removing the dish.

As the yeast grows and gives off carbon dioxide, the gas will collect in the top of the jar. Some of the solution will be forced out. ●

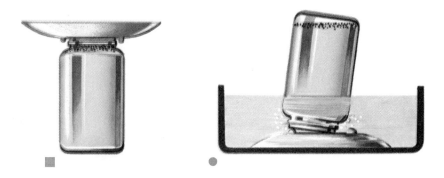

Now you have a way of observing the amount of carbon dioxide gas given off by growing yeast.

You can find out some interesting things about the environment of yeast. Will a solution with twice as much sucrose in it produce more gas? That is, will yeast grow more with more sugar? Will yeast grow more in four times as much sucrose? eight times as much? sixteen times as much? one half as much?

Is a sugar solution the best environment for yeast? Add a pinch of ammonium nitrate to a jar of sugar solution. Do nitrates improve the environment for the growth of yeast?

Will vitamins improve the environment?

Would a good scientist draw a conclusion from one or two observations?

How do you know it was the yeast that produced the carbon dioxide? Could it have been the sugar?

We are sure other questions will occur to you. You are on your own.

Beginning a Hobby

Many people pass a tree without knowing what kind it is. Yet trees can be very interesting. Trees are easy to identify in both summer and winter. Why not begin a study of trees? Become an expert on the trees of your neighborhood. You may find it fun.

A good way to start is to get one of these books. The pictures in them of trees, leaves, bark, and buds will give you a good start.

1. *Trees: A Guide to Familiar American Trees*, by Herbert S. Zim and Alexander C. Martin, published by Golden Press, 1956. Here is a book that will help you recognize over 100 different kinds of trees found in the United States.

2. *The First Book of Trees*, by Maribelle B. Cormack, published by Franklin Watts, New York, 1951. This book is useful to introduce you to the more common trees.

3. *Trees and Their World*, by Carroll L. Fenton and Dorothy C. Pallas, published by John Day Company, 1957. Although this book does not deal directly with identification, it will give you much useful information about trees.

These books are only a beginning. They will point to other ways of learning about trees.

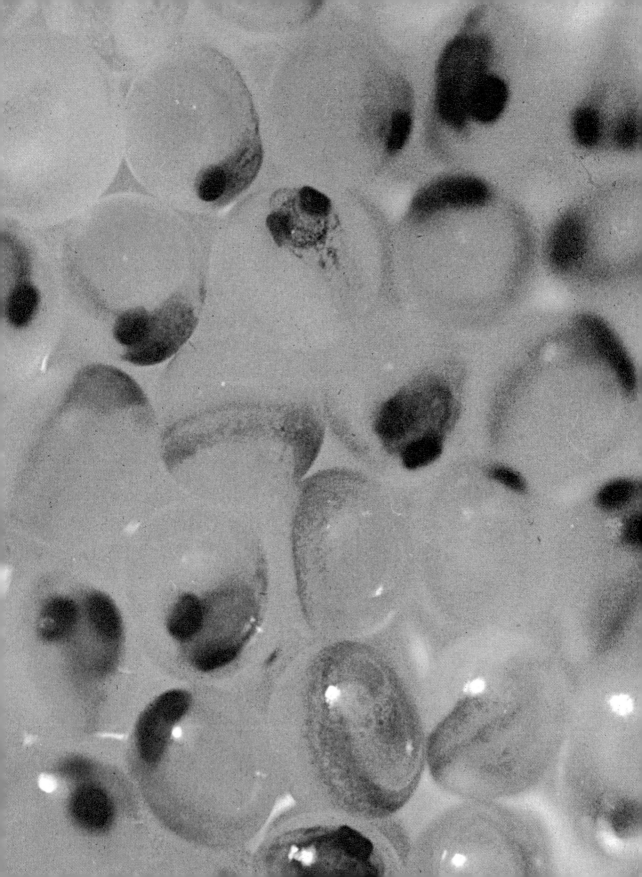

UNIT SIX

THE JOURNEYS OF A SALMON AND A DUCK

Do you know what these are?

These are the eggs of a fish—a salmon.
They lie at the bottom of a river in Oregon.

These eggs are the beginning of a strange life and a long journey. It is a journey which will take the young salmon thousands of miles away, and back here again.

Where do the salmon go? Why do they come back?

Let us find out.

1. In the Spring

The water in a river in Oregon is still very cold in the spring. It still has the feel of ice and snow from the winter that has just passed. It is hard to imagine that anything could live in that cold water.

Yet down on the bottom of the river, if you could explore there, you would find life beginning and thriving. In among the rocks and gravel on the river bottom, you would see these tiny creatures darting about. ■ If you explored still further, you

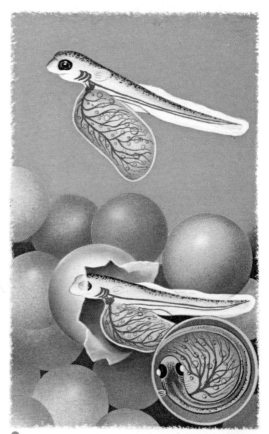

would find some hatching from eggs like these. ● At first they live on a food supply in the yolk sac. Later they feed on tiny plants and animals.

What are these creatures that can live and thrive in such surroundings? They are young salmon. How their eggs come to be in a cold river in Oregon is a strange story. Let us begin it by looking at the food that these young salmon find about them. This is something that you can see for yourself, in the investigation on the opposite page. `INVESTIGATE`

AN INVESTIGATION into a Food Supply

Needed: a stream, a pond, or an aquarium; a piece of hard-boiled egg yolk or some rice, four jars and covers, four labels, a hand lens or a microscope

Do this investigation in the spring, when the trees are beginning to show leaves. Scoop up a jar of clear water from a stream or pond, or from an aquarium. In a second jar scoop up water and some of the mud or gravel from the bottom.

Back in the classroom, pour half the contents of each jar into two other jars. Now you have four jars, two with clear water and two with water and mud or gravel.

Take a jar of clear water and a jar of mud or gravel and label them "Food added." Label the other two jars "No food added."

Into the jars labeled "Food added" put five grains of rice or a bit of hard-boiled egg yolk about the size of a pea. Crumble the egg yolk as it is added to the water. Put no egg yolk or rice in the jars labeled "No food added."

Keep all the jars loosely covered, in the classroom, away from heat and sunlight. Examine them every day. Here is one trial. ■ Which of the jars become cloudy? Why?

Additional Investigation: Examine the cloudy water under a hand lens or microsope. (Pages 289–94 explain how to use the microscope.) The tiny animals you will see are part of the food supply for many young fish.●

Examine the clear water under the microscope. Does this water have as many of these tiny animals? Why?

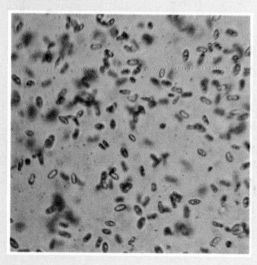

Food for Young Salmon

A jar of clear pond water seems to have no life in it. Then food is added to the water and life appears, tiny specks of animals moving about. How does this happen?

When egg yolk (or rice) is added to the water, you can see a change take place in the yolk from day to day. We say the yolk decays. The change takes place because tiny living things in the water are feeding on the yolk. These living things are very tiny plants called bacteria, as you will recall from your earlier work.

Bacteria are so small that they can be seen only with a good microscope.

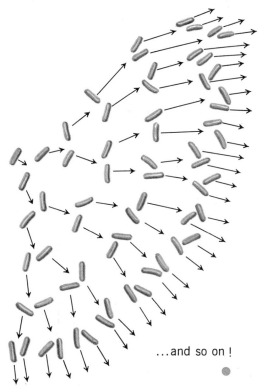

...and so on !

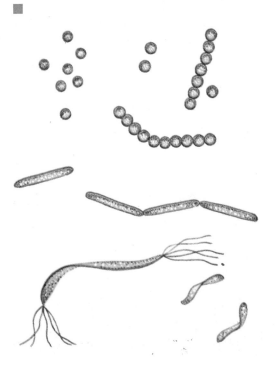

To your eye the pond water may seem clear. Here are some bacteria in pond water, as seen under the microscope. ■ Bacteria are so small that about 100,000 of them would fit into the period at the end of this sentence.

The bacteria feed on the egg yolk and the yolk decays. As the bacteria feed, they make more of themselves. One splits into two. Two bacteria become four. Four bacteria become eight. Eight become sixteen, and so on.● In a few days the clear water in the jar becomes cloudy, because of the millions upon millions of bacteria living in the water.

There are other living creatures in that clear pond water, though, besides bacteria. There are tiny single-celled green plants called **algae** (AL-jee). Algae are much larger than bacteria, but some types are still too small to be seen. There are also tiny single-celled animals, called **protozoans** (proh·teh·ZOH·enz). Here are some protozoans. ▲

The slipper-shaped protozoan that is first in line is called a *paramecium* (par·ah·MEE·shee·uhm). A paramecium is much larger than one of the bacteria. One hundred thousand bacteria of decay could fit into the period at the end of this sentence. Only five paramecia (the plural of *paramecium*) could fit there.

The paramecia feed on the bacteria. If there are plenty of bacteria, the paramecia make more of themselves. Each paramecium splits to make two paramecia. Those two split to make four paramecia, and so on. In a few days the jar of pond water is swarming with paramecia. The moving specks that can be seen with the hand lens are paramecia. There are also plenty of other tiny animals that you cannot see.

In your jar of pond water, the bacteria fed on egg yolk or rice. Then the paramecia fed on the bacteria. So did the other tiny animals.

Now let us go back to that river in Oregon. The salmon eggs on the bottom of the river have hatched. The young fish have used up all the food stored in their yolk sacs. What are they eating now? The tiny life—the algae, protozoans, and other tiny plant and animal life—are their food. The young fish are snapping up protozoans, other tiny animals, and algae. The protozoans

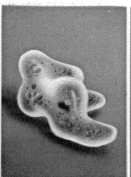

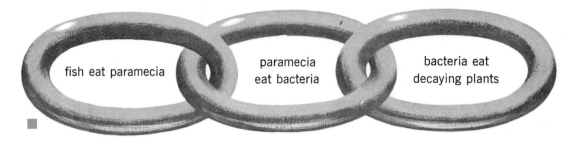

fish eat paramecia

paramecia eat bacteria

bacteria eat decaying plants

and other tiny animals are feeding on the bacteria in the water. The bacteria are feeding on bits of plants in the water. This is called a **food chain.**■

The young salmon was born in the right surroundings, wasn't it? At least it had a supply of food. Those salmon eggs were laid in the right place. The salmon that laid those eggs made a remarkable journey to lay them in just the right place. It was a long, long journey, and a dangerous one. Let us follow, in the next section you will study, a salmon on the journey to the right place to lay its eggs.

BEFORE YOU GO ON Study these statements and choose the correct responses. Your study will help fix in your mind the main concept of this section.

1. Paramecia produce other paramecia by
  a. hatching from eggs   b. dividing

2. The young salmon feeds not only on tiny animals but on tiny plants known as
  a. algae   b. protozoans

3. A young salmon is
  a. part of a food chain
  b. not part of a food chain

USING WHAT YOU KNOW **1.** Suppose that a paramecium can divide into two paramecia every 20 minutes. How many paramecia will there be in 2 hours?

2. Hawks eat snakes. Snakes feed on mice. Mice feed on grain. Draw the food chain.

3. Draw the food chain that begins with a decaying plant and ends with a young salmon.

ON YOUR OWN   Draw a food chain with *you* in it.

2. The Great Journey Begins

The Pacific Ocean is vast. It washes against our west coast from northern Alaska to southern California. ● From our coast it stretches thousands of miles to the west. In the Pacific Ocean are enormous numbers of living creatures, of many different kinds. There are the simplest animals, made up of just one cell. There are animals made up of many cells: sponges, worms, and relatives of the jellyfish, some that look like beautiful flowers. There are also crabs and lobsters of many kinds, and clams and other animals with shells. (One clamlike animal is the size of a small child.) There are octopuses and squids.

Then there are the fish. There are thousands of kinds of fish in the Pacific Ocean. Among them are the salmon.

Here are two full-grown Chinook salmon, a male and a female, about 4 years old. ■ Each weighs about 25 pounds and is nearly three feet long. The female salmon is ready to lay her eggs. She will not lay them in the Pacific Ocean, however. Where will she go?

When it is almost time to lay the eggs, both salmon begin a great journey. They begin to swim toward the land. Thousands of salmon in the Pacific Ocean do the same. Each salmon is heading for the river where it was born. Not only that, each salmon is heading for the very part of the river where it was hatched. A salmon may be a thou-sand miles from where it began life, yet it always heads for that place.

As the salmon swim, larger fish attack them. The salmon are food for some other fish. The salmon swim on. Some are caught by fishermen. The salmon that are left keep swim-ming. Their goal is far up the rivers that empty into the Pacific Ocean. As they swim, each salmon loses weight, because it feeds less and less.

What do the salmon do when they find a waterfall in their way? They leap up the waterfall, if it is not too high. Salmon can leap up a fall as high as ten feet. ● They leap by swimming at full speed under water, then rising to the surface. In some places the men of the United States Fish and Wildlife Service come to the aid of the salmon. Where the salmon cannot leap the falls, men have built **fish ladders.**  A fish ladder is a kind of stairs for fish to climb. The fish leap from one step to the next higher one. The fish ladder in the photograph allows the salmon to climb quite a height and reach the stream above the falls.

At a certain time in its life cycle, a salmon is adapted to life in a stream. At another time, it is adapted to life in the sea. The salmon behaves differently at different times of its life. The way it behaves is part of its adaptation to its environment.

At last the salmon that are left, at the end of this great journey, reach the places where they were hatched, far up the rivers. Some reach there in summer, others in the early autumn. They have come hundreds, even thousands of miles, and it has taken them weeks and months. They have survived many dangers. Here the salmon **spawn.** That is, the female salmon lays **eggs,** and the male salmon lays **sperm** over the eggs. For there to be young salmon, both eggs and sperm are needed. The place where the salmon do this is called their spawning ground.

At the spawning ground the female salmon lays from 8,000 to 10,000 eggs. Are these eggs just laid on the bottom of the stream? No, the salmon make a kind of nest. Before the eggs are laid, both salmon move along one place on the bottom, moving their heads and tails from side to side. They make a long hollow in the river bed. There the female lays the eggs. The eggs fall between the stones in the hollow. There they lie, protected by the stones, until they hatch.

This is the end of the journey for the old salmon. For the young in the eggs, it is the beginning.

The Young Salmon and Their Journey

You may have seen a guppy give birth to young fish. (The guppy is a fish you often see in home aquariums.) The male guppy is brightly colored. The female is olive colored. The female guppy does not lay eggs, as most fish do. The eggs hatch inside the guppy. Then, when the young fish are born, they are ready to swim about.

How different the salmon is from the guppy! The guppy does not lay eggs; the young are born from the female guppy. The salmon lays its eggs in a stony hollow. The eggs fall between the stones, so most of the eggs are protected. They are protected from other fish, that is; for salmon eggs are good food to other fish. There, among the stones, the eggs lie for a while. Nothing seems to be happening to the eggs.

What happens in a salmon egg while it is lying between the stones at the bottom of a river?

How a Salmon Egg Hatches

When a salmon egg drops between stones at the bottom of a river, the young salmon is already growing inside the egg. When the young salmon inside the egg reaches this size, it stops growing.● It remains inside the egg, not growing at all, during the long winter.

Then in early spring the young salmon begins to grow again. It forms a yolk sac. Now it is ready to hatch. The young salmon, yolk sac and all, bursts out of the egg.▲

This very young salmon is less than an inch long. It carries its food in the yolk sac, and lives on the

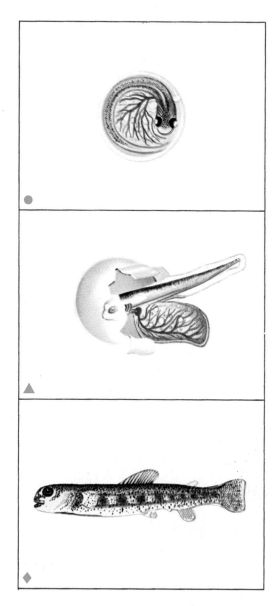

yolk for many weeks. By the time that the yolk is used up, the young salmon looks like this. ◆ Now it looks more like a fish, doesn't it? But with those spots and stripes, it does not look like a salmon. (In fact, people

used to think that it wasn't a salmon.) The young salmon is now called a parr.

The parr is fast and it has good teeth. It feeds on water insects and other small animals in the river. In 2 years it grows to be almost 8 inches long, if no enemies have caught up with it. No longer does it have red spots and stripes. The young salmon has a shiny, silvery coat. ■ Now the young salmon, two years old, is called a smolt.

Now that it is a smolt, the young fish is ready to go on a journey, a long journey to the ocean. It heads down the river. It reaches the mouth of the river, where the river water flows into the sea. The smolt heads out into the Pacific Ocean. There it lives for 2 years and becomes a full-grown salmon. In the Pacific it hunts for food and fights to protect itself. It is on guard against its enemies,

and ranges for hundreds of miles through the ocean depths. The salmon can do all these things because it is equipped to do them.

The adult male and female salmon came from the sea to the river. There they spawned. The young hatched from the eggs. The young grew and became smolts. The smolts headed for the sea and became adults.

This is the life cycle of the salmon. It is called a cycle because the life of the salmon is repeated over and over again. Young salmon become adults. Adult salmon produce young salmon. Those young salmon become adults . . . and so on. Our English word *cycle* comes from a Greek word meaning *circle*. A life cycle is a kind of circle of life. Do you see how the travels of the salmon is a life cycle?

It would be fine if you could get a salmon egg or two and watch them hatch. For most of us that is not possible, however. You *can* observe another kind of egg, a snail's egg. One way that salmon eggs are like snails' eggs is that both kinds have a clear jelly around them. This jelly protects the egg. You can observe some interesting things about eggs by doing the investigation on the opposite page. **INVESTIGATE**

AN INVESTIGATION into the Hatching of an Egg

Needed: a planted aquarium with snails in it, a hand lens, a dish, a medicine dropper

The snails pictured here came from an aquarium with many plants in it. This snail has a coiled shell.■ It lays eggs on the sides of the aquarium.● The snail with a spiral, pointed shell lays eggs on the underside of leaves.▲

The eggs are protected in a kind of jelly. They can be pulled off the surface they are clinging to or scraped off with the medicine dropper. Suck the eggs into the dropper, and place them in some aquarium water in the dish.

Examine the eggs every day with the hand lens. Observe when the snail begins to move in the egg. When does the snail leave the egg? How does it get out? When the tiny snails hatch, feed them bits of lettuce.

Additional Investigation: Although the frog and salmon belong to two different groups of animals, their eggs hatch in somewhat the same way. Frog eggs are laid in early spring. If you can get frog eggs, observe how they hatch. In what ways do they hatch very much as the salmon eggs do? In what ways do they hatch differently?

 ■

 ●

 ▲

Study these statements and choose the correct responses. Your study will help fix in your mind the main concept of this section.

1. Salmon lay their eggs in the
   a. sea   b. river

2. When salmon spawn, the male salmon produces
   a. eggs   b. sperm

3. The young salmon just hatched lives on
   a. yolk   b. food it catches

1. What kinds of animals live in the environment of the adult salmon?

2. What is a fish ladder, and what is it for?

3. How does the salmon develop after it hatches?

4. Put these words and phrases in order so that they show the life cycle of the salmon.

smolt	down to the sea
eggs	spawning
parr	adult salmon
up the river	

In the Library

The eel has a life cycle somewhat like the salmon, with one great difference. Look up the life cycle of the eel. Part of the story is on page 205. For further reference the library will help.

3. To the Ocean and Back

A salmon is a beautiful animal. It is built for the work of swimming in the ocean. It is fitted for living in its watery surroundings. Remember that the surroundings of a living thing are called environment. The salmon is fitted for living in its special environment, or **habitat** (HAB·ih-tat). A habitat is the special environment in which an animal lives. For instance, a mole lives underground. Its special environment, or habitat, is underground.

The Fitness of Salmon

A fish is fitted to live in its environment of water in many ways. The fish can move about in order to hunt and to hide. It can breathe. It can get food and eat it.

When a living thing is fitted to an environment, we say it is *adapted* to the environment. An oak tree is adapted to its environment. The goldfish is adapted to its environment. The salmon is adapted to its environment.

There is a difference between the environment of a goldfish and a salmon. The goldfish would die in seawater. The special environment, the habitat, of a goldfish is a pond, not the sea. A grown salmon would die in a pond. Its special environment, or habitat, is the sea.

Even if the environment of all fish is water, each fish has a special habitat. In that habitat it finds its special food. An eagle cannot live on grass. A cow cannot live on mice. Each kind of living thing has its own habitat, with its own food. Each living thing is adapted to its habitat. ■

■

How is a salmon fitted to its habitat? You can investigate this problem with the help of a goldfish, as shown on the next page. `INVESTIGATE`

AN INVESTIGATION into the Fitness of a Fish

Needed: a fish (a goldfish will do) in an aquarium

Observe the fish as it swims about. Study it closely, and see how many

things you can notice about the fish.

How is the fish fitted for moving through water? How does it swim? How does it turn? How does it go up or down?

The fish's scales are a part of its fitness for living in water. How are the scales placed?

How is the fish fitted for getting oxygen? Does the fish keep its mouth closed or open? There are openings just in back of the fish's head. How do they move? Do they seem to have anything to do with the fish's mouth? You may be able to see inside these openings as the fish moves them. What can you see?

Additional Investigation: Watch the fish at feeding time. How is the fish fitted for getting food?

Look at the salmon's adaptations for moving about. Look at the salmon's muscles. ■ Notice how they make a kind of zigzag pattern. Almost the whole body of a salmon is made of muscle. (When you eat salmon, you eat muscle, mainly.) It is these powerful muscles that make the salmon fit for fast swimming, turning quickly, and leaping high out of the water. The powerful tail drives the salmon along. The two chest fins are for steering. See how the body is streamlined, like the shape of a fast airplane. With this shape the body moves more easily through the water.

Notice another part of the salmon's equipment, its shiny scales. They lap over each other like shingles on a roof. Strangely enough, scales have much the same job as shingles. Scales keep water out of a fish's body. If they did not, the fish would take in too much water through its skin. Like a piece of wood that has been soaked in water the fish might become waterlogged.

Let us look at one more part of the salmon's equipment that fits the salmon for living in its environment. The salmon not only gets food from water, it gets oxygen from water. This is something you cannot do, no matter how hard you try. Let us see how a fish does it.

Oxygen from Water

Thoroughly boil a gallon of water. Let it cool, then put a goldfish in

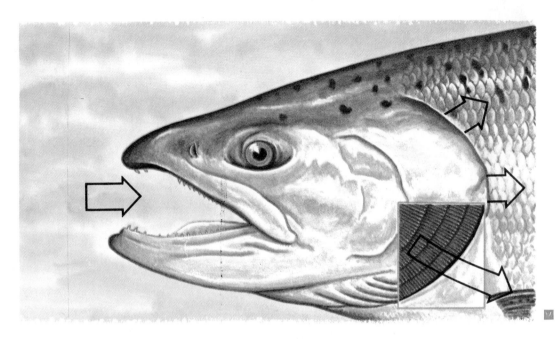

it. An odd thing happens. A gold-fish is fitted to live in water, yet a goldfish in cooled boiled water does not seem at ease. Soon the goldfish comes to the surface. It puts its head out of the water to swallow air. Why?

By boiling the water, most of the dissolved oxygen in the water is driven out. Oxygen, remember, is a gas. It dissolves in water in the same way that sugar dissolves in water. Ordinary water has plenty of dis-solved oxygen in it. It is this dissolved oxygen that a fish uses. Boiled water has little oxygen in it, and the fish comes to the surface to get oxygen from the air. It is a good idea to put the goldfish back in its regular

water when this happens, for it is not adapted to get enough oxygen from the air to live.

You have probably observed a fish under water opening and clos-ing its mouth, as if it were swallow-ing something. The fish is taking in water through its mouth. It sends this water through its **gills.** ■ The gills are a fish's equipment for tak-ing oxygen out of water. In the gills dissolved oxygen passes out of the water and into the blood of the fish. The oxygen is carried by the blood to every part of the fish. The gills do for a fish what your lungs do for you: they supply oxygen. Lungs take oxygen from air. Gills take oxy-gen from water.

There are many other ways in which a salmon is adapted to its environment. After 2 years in the environment of the Pacific Ocean, the salmon that were smolts have become full grown. They are ready for the great journey back to the rivers where they were hatched.

The Return

Now the large, fierce, shining salmon that have roamed the Pacific Ocean for 2 years begin to turn toward the shore, toward the rivers they swam down 2 years before. They are returning to the rivers and streams where they were born. More and more salmon start the return. Soon thousands upon thousands of salmon are swimming through the ocean, headed for the rivers that run to the sea. Their strong, muscular bodies help them to swim fast, without stopping.

They enter the rivers and head upstream. Where rocks and falls break the waters, the salmon leap over them. Sometimes the salmon leap many feet to the next level of the water. They do not stop to feed. They swim and swim. At last they reach the spawning ground in a high, cold mountain stream. All along the Pacific Coast from Oregon to Alaska, salmon return to spawn. They are thin and ragged. They spawn, the females laying their eggs and the males pouring sperm over them. The eggs settle to the bottom of the river.

The big salmon are finished. After they spawn, still they do not feed. They die. Their bodies are washed downstream. They serve as food for other fish.

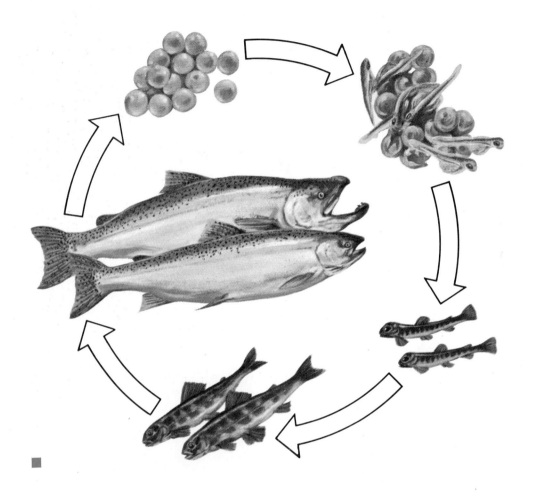

Back upstream, between the rocks, rest the salmon eggs. They will hatch when spring comes. The young salmon with their yolk sacs will burst from the eggs. The spotted parr will flash about in the stream. Then the smolt will head out to sea. The life cycle of the salmon goes on. ■

Notice that a life cycle has no ending. It goes on and on. Every living thing has a life cycle. Snakes and frogs and ferns have a life cycle. Oak trees have a life cycle, as you learned in Unit Five. Birds have life cycles, too, as you will soon discover, in studying the next section.

BEFORE
YOU GO ON Study these statements and choose the correct responses. Your study will help fix in your mind the main concept of this section.

1. A special environment in which living things are found is known as a

    a. habitat   b. food chain

2. The life cycle of the salmon

    a. ends at death   b. goes on and on

3. The life cycle of the salmon is adapted to

    a. any environment

    b. a special environment

USING WHAT
YOU KNOW **1.** A goldfish and a salmon have different habitats. How are they different?

2. A cow and an eagle have different habitats. How are they different?

3. A man and a whale have different habitats. How are they different?

4. In what ways is the salmon not adapted to a land environment?

ON YOUR OWN How does the habitat of a moss differ from that of a cactus?

4. Salmon and Wild Duck

Salmon fight their way up rivers. In the fall the salmon eggs lie on the river bottoms between the rocks. There they stay during the cold winter.

In the spring the eggs hatch. In 2 years the young salmon head down the rivers toward the sea. For 2 years they live in the sea and become full grown. Then they return to the rivers where they were born. They lay their eggs among the river stones. The cycle goes on. This is the life cycle of the salmon.

The salmon is fitted to this life. It is adapted to its environment. The life cycle of the salmon is really a story of how the salmon is adapted to its environment, isn't it? The story is unusual. Yet the concept of living things being adapted to their environment is not unusual at all. After all, you are adapted to your environment.

Notice that the entire life cycle of the salmon, from eggs to adult to eggs, is adapted for life in the ocean and the river. The whole life cycle of a living thing is adapted to its environment.

There are many, many different life cycles. Let us follow another life cycle. Let us look at the life cycle of a land animal this time—a wild duck.

A Flight of Ducks

Dawn is just starting to shed a pale light over a northern lake, after a cold night. It is early spring. The ice on the lake is beginning to break. It is quiet. A small moving smudge appears in the sky, far off. It gets nearer and bigger. It is a group of wild ducks, flying fast, beating the air with short, strong wings, necks outstretched, feet tucked up, all streamlined. Down they come out of the sky to land on the icy water. This is the end of their journey. ■

Where have they come from? A thousand miles away, in the south.

Wild ducks are real travelers. In the fall, six months ago, they had flown south for the winter months. Year after year wild ducks fly south in the fall and fly north in the spring.

What will they do now that they have come back? Let us look at some of the things they will do.

Near the shores of the lake, among the reeds, the ducks begin to build nests. They are mallard ducks. ●

Like most birds, the male mallard has different coloring from the female. (In the picture, the male mallard is the more colorful one.) The mallards build their nest with leaves and grass and line it with down. Down is the soft, fluffy feathers that grow under the duck's ordinary feathers.

When the nest is built, the female duck lays from six to ten brown eggs in it. Then she sits on the eggs, warming them until they hatch.

You have eaten eggs many times, of course. But have you ever *studied* an egg to see how it fits into the life cycle of the bird? Study a hen's egg. In the investigation on the next page you can do so. **INVESTIGATE**

AN INVESTIGATION into a Bird's Egg

Needed: a hen's egg, a dish, a hand lens

Examine the eggshell with the hand lens. Is it glazed, like a china dish, or is it porous? A porous shell has tiny holes in it that let air through. ■

Crack the shell gently. Peel off a chip or two of the shell and notice the skin, or **membrane,** beneath it.● Air can pass through this membrane.

Open the egg and empty it into the dish without breaking the yolk. With the hand lens, find the white speck on the yolk.▲ This speck joins with the sperm and forms the **embryo** (EM·bree·oh), or beginning, of the young bird. While the egg is kept warm, the embryo grows inside the shell. In about 21 days, the chick hatches.

Additional Investigation: What does the growing embryo use as food?

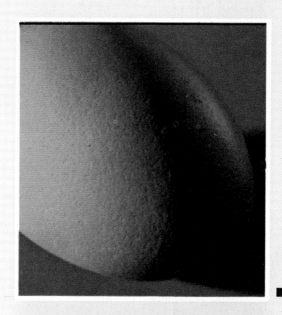

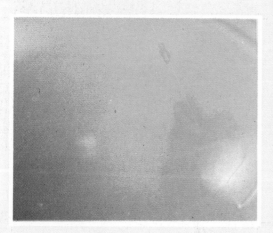

1. Millions of years ago, dinosaurs were found in many places on land. Then the environment changed, but the dinosaurs did not change. They died out.

Can you use the concept of adaptation to explain the dying out of the dinosaurs?

2. How is the duck adapted to flight?

3. How is the duck adapted for hatching its young out of the egg?

4. How is the egg adapted to the life of the embryo?

5. The Life Cycle of a Duck

The egg of the mallard duck is much like a hen's egg. Its shell is not glazed, but porous. There is a membrane just under the shell, a thin, white skin. There is an egg white, and a yellow yolk inside it. And there is a speck on the yolk that is the beginning of the embryo. The embryo uses the white and the yolk for food while it is growing in the shell.

Toward the end of its time inside the shell, the duck embryo looks like this.■ You can already recognize wings and eyes and other parts.

Just hatched, the duckling can soon walk and feed itself.● Is it much different from the adult ducks? In a year it will begin to get the look and the feathers of an adult duck.

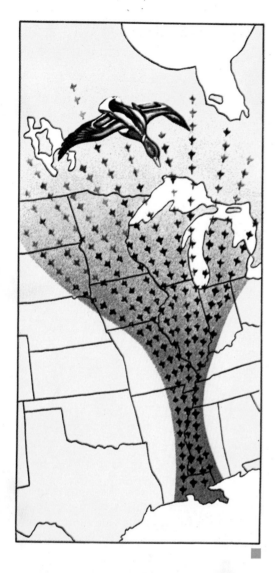

the young salmon carries a yolk sac for almost 6 weeks. Its food is in the sac. But when a young duck hatches, it has used up all the food stored in its egg. The young duck is ready to look for its own food.

To grow from a downy duckling to a handsome duck, the mallard must eat, of course. Like other ducks, mallards like to eat grain, such as wild rice. However, they will eat small frogs, toads, lizards, small fish, snails, earthworms, and even mice. They will eat nuts and acorns, fruits, and many water plants. What a diet! Because ducks can eat so many different things, they can live in many different parts of the country.

Think of this for a moment, too. Whatever a duck eats, it takes from its environment. Whatever a duck eats, the duck's body uses to make itself grow. Everything a duck eats turns into duck.

The Long Journey

Let us look again at those mallard ducks nesting by that northern lake. The mallards are in their breeding grounds, the places where they build their nests and lay eggs. They flew into the breeding grounds in the early spring, you remember. There was still ice on the lake.

The young of some birds, such as robins and eagles, must be fed by the parents at first. The young of dogs and cats and horses must be fed. So must the young of human beings. But not ducklings! Notice the difference between a salmon and a duck. When a salmon egg hatches,

As spring turns to summer, the ducklings have been growing. By fall they can fly well. They need to fly, for one day in early winter, when ice is beginning to cover the lake, the whole flock rises into the air and heads south. Flocks of ducks fill the sky, going south and east, where food is plentiful, 2,000 miles away.

One long journey of the ducks is shown on this map. ■ They spend the winter months in the south and east. Then in late winter or early spring they fly back to their breeding grounds in the north and west. This kind of traveling back and forth is called **migration** (my·GRAY-sh'n). Ducks migrate in the fall, and they migrate again in the spring.

This is the life cycle of the duck. ●

How Do They Know?

Ducks fly more than 2,000 miles to their breeding grounds. Then they fly back again. How do ducks know where and when to fly?

How does a salmon know which river to return to, and when to return?

How do ducks know what kind of nest to build? All mallards build the same kind of nest, even the very first time they build one.

When a duckling sees a hawk for the first time, the duckling does not hesitate. It dives into the water at once and hides among the water weeds. How does a duckling know that a hawk is its enemy?

A female duck will try to lead an enemy away from where its ducklings are hiding. How does the mother know that she should do this, the first time she has young?

How do animals know these things? Do young ducks learn them from their mother? Do young salmon learn from their parents? Or is there some other way by which animals know how to escape an enemy or how to protect their young? Do they have to be taught?

Study these statements and choose the correct responses. Your study will help fix in your mind the main concept of this section.

1. Migration of ducks takes place at
   a. any time   b. a certain time

2. Ducks lay their eggs in the
   a. northern regions   b. southern regions

3. The life cycle of a duck is fitted to
   a. any environment
   b. a special environment

1. A young duck just hatched can begin to feed itself. Can it take care of itself? Is the young duck completely adapted to its environment?

2. What is one important difference between a young salmon (just hatched) and a young duck (just hatched)?

In the Library
Other birds besides the mallard duck migrate. Select a bird like a swallow, goose, or golden plover. Make a map of its migration. The library will help.

6. Knowing How to Behave

The salmon have their life cycle. The ducks have their life cycle. The young salmon swim out to sea, but return to the rivers to lay their eggs. The young ducks fly south but return, for example, to the northwestern United States to lay their eggs. How do they know how to do these things?

To get a clue to the answer, start with a growing bean. Try the investigation on the opposite page. INVESTIGATE

AN INVESTIGATION into the Behavior of a Bean

Needed: four jars, four pieces of blue blotting paper, twelve dried bean seeds

Soak the dried beans overnight in water, to make them ready to grow. The water should just cover the beans.

Place three of the soaked beans in each jar, between a piece of blotting paper and the glass. ■ Soak the blotter with water. Examine the blotter every day to be sure that it is moist. Soak it again if needed.

Now place the jars in four different positions. Stand one right side up. Stand another upside down. Lay another on its side. Place the last jar so that it is tilted.

Observe the beans every day.

In which direction do the roots grow? In which direction do the stems grow?

Does the position of the bean make a difference?

Here is what happened in one trial. ●

Do you think the beans had to learn how to behave this way?

Additional Investigation: Try this same investigation with corn. Does corn behave the same way?

Earth. This is the way bean plants behave, isn't it? In fact, the roots of most green plants grow down, and the stems grow up. This is the **behavior** of most green plants. This is the behavior of a bean plant. ■

How is a bean plant able to do this? We are sure that a bean does not learn to behave this way. Beans cannot learn. Learning is not the answer. The answer is that the bean's behavior is built into the bean. The behavior is born in the bean, or in other words, the behavior is **inborn.** This behavior is part of a bean from the moment it becomes a bean. Like its color, its shape, and its size, the behavior of the bean is inborn.

How?

The roots of a bean plant grow toward the Earth. The stem of the bean plant grows away from the

Let us look at another kind of behavior. Perhaps you have seen moths flying around a light. Again and again they bounce against the glass. They cannot seem to get away. Most moths that fly at night are attracted by light and fly toward it. They behave this way from the time they are hatched. This behavior is part of the moth from its birth. It is inborn. It is not learned.

The spider making this web has not learned how to do this.● The behavior of making a web is a part of the spider from birth. All the spiders of this kind make this kind of web. This behavior is also inborn. It is not learned.

It is the same with nest-building in birds. Birds separated from their parents from birth make the same kinds of nests as the parent birds. All eastern robins make the same kind of nest.▲ All Baltimore orioles make the same kind of nest. ◆ All mallards make the same kind of nest. Nest-building is inborn behavior.

Mallards migrate. So do other kinds of birds: robins, wild geese, and many song birds. Salmon migrate. So do other kinds of fish. Along the Atlantic Coast the shad, a salt-water fish, migrates into fresh-water rivers to spawn.

Eels in rivers along the east coast have an interesting life cycle. Eels are hatched in warm waters in the Atlantic Ocean. The young migrate when they are about one year old. They enter fresh-water rivers where they live for six or seven years. Then they migrate to the warm Atlantic to spawn. Salmon, too, migrate, as you have learned.

Birds and fishes do not learn to migrate. Migration is a kind of behavior that is inborn.

When?

In the spring, salmon start swimming to the sea. In early spring, mallards start flying to the northwest. How does a fish or a bird know *when* to migrate?

Scientists have investigated this question. For example, scientists did some investigations with the birds pictured here, called juncos (JUNG-kohz). ■ Juncos migrate. They begin to fly north in the spring. Scientists wondered if they could make some juncos migrate earlier than usual. If they could, they might have a clue to what made juncos migrate at a certain time.

You know that the days get longer as we go from winter to spring. Some scientists suspected that the length of the days might have something to do with when juncos migrated. So some juncos were kept in barns. Lights in the barns were turned on and off to control the length of "day" in the barns. When the days became about 8 hours long, the juncos began to get ready to migrate. When the days became about 10 hours long, the juncos began to migrate.

It was the number of hours of daylight that set off the juncos' migration. The amount of daylight seemed to be the **stimulus** (STIM-yoo·lus) for migration. A stimulus is anything that produces a **response,** or answer. A bright light is a stimulus which attracts moths. The flight of the moths toward the light is their response. When you respond to hearing your name called, you are responding to a stimulus. You may respond by doing something when your name is called.

When the length of the day reaches a certain number of hours, it is a stimulus for juncos. The juncos respond to this stimulus by migrating. Mallards begin to migrate when the days are about 8 hours long. Other kinds of birds may migrate at other times. Different birds are adapted to migrate at different times. Each kind of bird is adapted to its environment.

Each kind of fish is adapted to its environment, too. When the ocean water in which the salmon swims reaches a certain temperature, the salmon begins to migrate. The salmon is adapted to its environment.

All living things are adapted to their environment.

BEFORE YOU GO ON
Study these statements and choose the correct responses. Your study will help fix in your mind the main concept of this section.

1. A moth flies toward a light. We expect that this behavior is
   a. learned   b. inborn

2. The migration of a duck is
   a. learned   b. inborn

3. A stimulus leads to
   a. a response   b. another stimulus

USING WHAT YOU KNOW
1. What kind of inborn behavior do you expect from the stems of plants? How is this different from the inborn behavior of the roots?

2. What evidence is there that nest-building in birds is not learned?

3. Do *you* have any inborn acts? What is the evidence that they are inborn?

ON YOUR OWN   Do you know of any animal or plant that is adapted to *all* environments?

7. The Main Concept: Adaptation to Environment

You have studied the strange behavior of salmon and ducks, the strange behavior called migration.

Is it right to call this behavior "strange" now? This behavior is the way of life for the Pacific salmon and for the mallard duck. Their migration behavior is inborn. Salmon and duck are adapted in this way to their environment from the moment that they hatch.

Notice that adaptation has two sides to it. One side is adaptation by structure. The salmon is adapted by the structure of its body to live in water. Its gills enable it to get the oxygen dissolved in water. Its fins enable it to swim in water. Its body cuts a path through the water easily. The salmon is not adapted to flight in air; the duck is. Structure helps adapt a living thing to its environment.

But structure is not the only thing that helps adapt a living thing to its environment. A living thing is also adapted to its environment by its behavior. For instance, migration is one kind of behavior. Adaptation is helped by the behavior of a living thing, as well as by its structure.

Do not think that all behavior of a fish or a bird is inborn. A bird or a fish can learn some things. A fish, for instance, can learn to come to one corner of its tank for food. It may learn *when* to come, too.

This keeper is feeding a dolphin (a mammal of the sea) in an aquarium in Florida. ■ Even before the keeper comes to feed it, the dolphin waits at the place where it is fed. This behavior is not inborn. It is learned.

From what scientists know now, the behavior of migration is inborn.

However, scientists are still studying migration. It is possible that they may discover that some part of the behavior of migration is learned. Just the same, this behavior is part of the life cycle of these living things. Migration is an example of how salmon and ducks are adapted by their behavior to the environment in which they live.

A Pacific salmon is hatched in a river, grows, and goes out to sea. A few years later it returns to the same river and lays its eggs. The salmon has completed its life cycle. This life cycle adapts the salmon to its environment. A mallard flies northward, more than 3,000 miles, to lay its eggs. Each year the duck makes this flight to continue its life cycle. This life cycle adapts the duck to its environment.

Salmon and ducks are living things. Like all living things, they are adapted to their environments. What is more, they are adapted to special habitats within their environment. Adaptation to their environment makes living things part of the life and land and water around them.

Fixing the Main Concepts

Study the statements below and choose the correct responses. Your study will help fix in your mind the main concepts of this unit.

1. A salmon hatches from an egg in
   a. a stream   b. the ocean

2. A smolt makes a journey toward
   a. a stream   b. the ocean

3. Male and female salmon become adults in
   a. a stream   b. the ocean

4. Male and female salmon journey back to
   a. a stream   b. the ocean

5. A duck begins its life, hatching from the egg, in
   a. northern lands   b. southern lands

6. The embryo shown in the picture below is a young
   a. fish   b. bird

7. The fitness of a duck for flight is known as
   a. migration   b. adaptation

8. The structure of a fish adapts it to take dissolved oxygen from

    a. water   b. air

9. The structure of living things adapts them to their habitats. This is true of

    a. all living things   b. animals only

FOR YOUR READING

1. *Animal Life and Lore,* by Osmond P. Breland, published by Harper & Row, New York, 1963. Here are answers to many questions about animals and their ways, from "How does a cat purr?" to "What is the most dangerous animal in the world?" There are lively and informative essays on many different creatures, as well.

2. *Honker, the Story of a Wild Goose,* by Robert M. Mc-Clung, published by William Morrow and Company, 1965. You find out about the life cycle of a wild goose as you follow the story of Honker.

3. *Insects and the Homes They Build,* by Dorothy Sterling, published by Doubleday and Company, Garden City, N. Y., 1954. Insects sometimes adapt to the environment by building shelters or traps, such as cocoons, honeycombs, and webs. This book is a good account of adaptations of living things.

4. *Red Tag Comes Back,* by Frederick B. Phleger, published by Harper & Row, 1961. This is the exciting story of Red Tag, the salmon. It tells how she makes her long journey back to where she was born. There she lays her eggs, beginning again a new cycle of life.

5. *Winter-Sleeping Wildlife,* by Will Barker, published by Harper & Row, New York, 1958. This is an interesting account of the many ways of adaptation of wildlife to environment. You may particularly want to study hibernation, the winter-sleeping adaptation of bears and other animals.

1. Living things are adapted to their environment by means of their *structure* and their *behavior*. The gills and fins of the salmon adapt it to live in water. The wings of the duck adapt it to flight in air. The behavior of both salmon and duck adapt them to a change in habitat.

Can fish adapt to a *sudden* change in the environment? Perhaps you have an aquarium in your classroom. For this investigation it must contain at least two fish — or better yet, two kinds of fish. If you have tropical fish, you might use guppies and zebras, or two other types. The fish should have been in the aquarium for some time.

Separate the two types of fish in the aquarium with a glass plate. Your teacher will help get a piece of glass cut so that it will fit. Devise a way to support the glass plate so you have two separate compartments.

What happens? How do you explain the fishes' behavior?

2. Do you know that moths have an interesting life cycle with a strange adaptation? At a certain time in their life cycle, moths change form and go into a type of hibernation called a

diapause (DY·uh·pawse). During this period they form cocoons, such as these.■

Many boys and girls have taken up the hobby of collecting cocoons. They care for the moths which come from the cocoons and mate the moths to get eggs. A good way to begin is to read *Collecting Cocoons,* by Lois J. Hussey and Catherine Pessino, published by Thomas Y. Crowell, New York, 1953.

This book describes the life cycle of moths, and how to collect cocoons. There are instructions on how to care for moths as well.

In the study of cocoons, you will study the life cycles of some very interesting organisms. What stage of the life cycle of a moth is shown below?● To find out, look through a book like *Butterflies and Moths* by Robert T. Mitchell and Herbert S. Zim, published by Golden Press, 1964.

●

A New View of Living Things

We expect a bean seed to produce a bean plant, not a corn plant. We expect elephants to reproduce elephants, not horses. A duck's egg is expected to produce a duckling, not a chick.

Why do we expect each living thing to reproduce its own kind? Because we know that parents pass on their own characteristics to their young. The acorn of a white oak produces a white oak tree, not a red oak tree, because the parent tree passed on to that acorn the characteristics of a white oak. It is a duckling that pecks its way out of a duck egg because the parents pass on those characteristics. Living things reproduce their own kind. ∎

If . . .

Living things reproduce their own kind. There is an "if," however.

Suppose that a mallard duck laid its eggs in a cold stream where salmon lay their eggs. You can guess what would happen to the duck eggs. They would not develop. Nor would the salmon eggs develop if they were laid in a place that became dry. A living thing cannot reproduce anywhere. It must have a special environment for its young to develop. In fact, a living thing is adapted to a special environment.

Think of a fish and a duck. ● Each is adapted to a special environment. The fish gets its oxygen from water. The fish is adapted to get oxygen in this way by means of its gills. The duck gets its oxygen from the air. The duck is adapted for this by means of its lungs. Fish or duck, each is adapted to a special environment.

It is no different with plants. Why shouldn't a white oak seedling and a staghorn sumac seedling grow in the same place? After all, both have stems and leaves and roots. Yet the white oak grows best where soil is moist. The staghorn sumac grows best where soil is dry. Each has its own best environment. A small difference in that environment, as it seems to us, may mean the difference between good growth and poor growth—or none at all. (This is just as true for you as for white oaks and sumacs.)

Changing Environment

A living thing is adapted to a special environment, but this doesn't mean that the environment is always the same. Some living things adapt themselves to a different environment at certain times. Think of the life cycle of the salmon, for example. ■

At a certain time in its life, an adult salmon is adapted to living in the fresh water of a stream. It does not lay its eggs in the sea. The eggs develop only in the environment of the stream. So do the young salmon. Then, at a certain time, the young salmon changes its environment. It goes to the sea. There it grows to be an adult. But to complete its life cycle, it migrates again in a long and difficult journey back to the stream where it was born. It cannot complete its life cycle unless it does this. It is completely adapted to two different environments.

A Part of the Environment

Living things reproduce their own kind.

Living things are adapted to their environment.

These are two important and broad concepts, certainly, for they apply to every living thing. With these concepts in mind, you can look at *any* living thing and understand that living thing better.

There is one more concept.

Do you recall what the young salm-

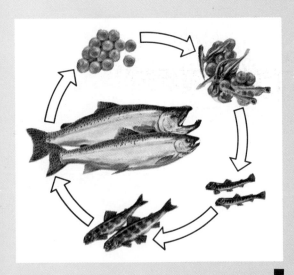

■

on ate as food?● The young salmon fed on water insects and other smaller animals in the river in which it lived. These smaller living things, then, which the young salmon ate, were a necessary part of the young salmon's environment.

You may remember, however, that the young salmon's life was a risky one. For other living things, larger than the young salmon, fed upon the young salmon. For these larger fish, the young salmon was a part of *their* environment. (We feed on salmon, too.)

So the young salmon was not only adapted to a certain special environment, but it was a part of the environment itself. This is true of all living things. Living things are not just adapted to life in a special environment. Living things are part of the environment.

The white oak growing in the woods is adapted to that special environment. But it is also a part of that environment itself. When it falls and dies, fungi and bacteria feed upon it; it decays and becomes part of the soil. Other seeds grow in what was once a tree.

Living things not only depend on their environment. Living things are part of it.

THE TRAVELS OF A HANDFUL OF SOIL

These are the Rocky Mountains. That tall peak reaches over two and one half miles high. The mountains are made of hard rock.

They look as if they would never change, don't they? They look as if they had always been there and would always be there.

But they have not always been there. They will not always be there. In fact, they are breaking down now.

How can this be? The Earth is always changing. Let us see how. We begin not with a mountain, but with a handful of soil.

1. The Moving Land

Here is a handful of soil. ■ Looking at it, you would not think of soil as a traveler, would you? Yet soil does travel, and sometimes, for amazing distances.

How does soil travel? Where does it travel to? Try the investigation on the opposite page and see for yourself. INVESTIGATE

A Model River

The pile of sand in the investigation became a model, a model of a river. The model river is very small compared to a real river. Yet it does show what can happen in a real river.

The model river shows that sand can be carried along by running water. At the bottom of the model hill is a pile of sand that has been carried down by the water. You may even have been able to see sand being carried along in the moving water.

This is not really surprising, is it? You know that running water has energy and can make things move. Running water can carry sand along. It can also carry soil. If it is moving fast enough, running water can carry stones and even boulders along. You may have seen how water carries soil after a rain. Perhaps you have seen it carry pebbles, too.

AN INVESTIGATION
into How Water Moves Land

Needed: an empty aquarium, coarse sand, a sprinkling can filled with water

Pile the sand at one end of the aquarium to make a hill. ■ Make a groove down the hill an inch or two deep. Make a clear area at the bottom of the hill, on the floor of the aquarium.

Take the watering can and sprinkle water gently on the hill to make "rain." Let water run down the groove so as to make a stream flowing down the hillside. ●

What happens to some of the sand that the water flows over? Where does that sand go?

Here is what happened on one trial. ▲

Additional Investigation: Is the water flowing fast or slow when it is carrying sand along?

Is the water flowing fast or slow when it drops the sand?

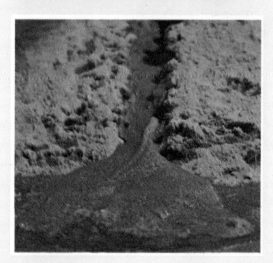

Look at this real river, keeping in mind what happened in the model river. ■ Can you imagine what happens to the soil around this river when it rains?

The rain washes the soil into the river. When it rains hard, much soil is washed into the river. Stones fall in, too. The soil and stones are carried along by the running water. See how muddy this river is. ● The water is muddy because it is carrying much soil. Some of this soil was washed into the river not far from here. Some of the soil entered the river hundreds of miles away and has been carried down. It is still traveling. It will keep on traveling until the river moves so slowly that the soil drops to the bed of the river.

How does soil travel? In running water. Where does it travel to? Wherever the water travels. What will happen to it? We shall see.

The land that appears so quiet and unmoving is really moving, isn't it? The handful of soil you pick up one day may be washed down a river later on. It may even travel to the bottom of the sea.

■

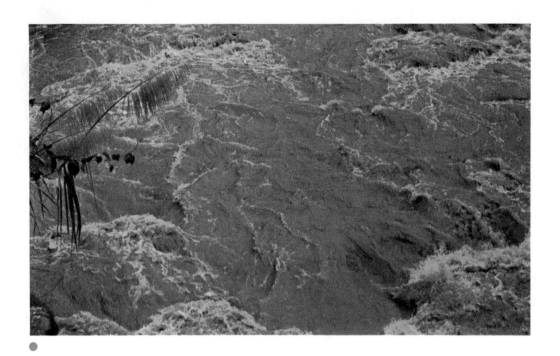

BEFORE YOU GO ON Study these statements and choose the correct responses. Your study will help fix in your mind the main concept of this section.

1. Running water can carry soil because it has
   a. energy   b. wetness

2. The faster water runs, the
   a. less soil it can carry   b. more soil it can carry

3. The faster water travels, the
   a. larger the stones it can carry
   b. smaller the stones it can carry

USING WHAT YOU KNOW

1. What does it mean when the water of a river is muddy?

2. Where do the soil and rock that are carried by a river come from?

3. What is another way in which soil may travel?

ON YOUR OWN   Suppose that a river is carrying along heavy particles, as well as light particles of soil and sand. What do you think will happen to the particles if the water slows down?

2. Rocks Break Down

Rain can wash soil away. It can wash small stones away as well. Streams and rivers may carry small stones and soil away, but the big rocks are left behind. Rain cannot carry away a mountain of rock.

Yet the big rocks, even the mountains of rock, are being moved.

Look at this evidence. Here is a photograph of a mountain in Colorado. Like all mountains, it is made of rock. Observe the pile of material heaped up against the mountain. What do you suppose it is? How did it get there? The material piled against the mountain is bits of broken rock. Bits of rock have broken off the mountain and have fallen down its slopes. The mountain is being broken to pieces.

What could be strong enough to break down a mountain? The investigation on the opposite page will help you to find out.   INVESTIGATE

AN INVESTIGATION into Freezing Water

Needed: an empty can with its top removed, a freezer or refrigerator, water

Fill the can with water so that the surface of the water is just level with the top of the can. ■

Place the can of water in the freezer, or in the freezing compartment of the refrigerator. ●

Freeze the water. As the water becomes ice, what happens to the room it takes up?

Here is what happened in one trial. ▲ How do you explain what happened?

Additional Investigation: As the water in the can froze, did it take up more room or less room? By how much did it change in size? Design your own investigation to measure this change.

The Force of Ice

When water freezes, it takes up more room. In other words, it expands. When a quart of water freezes, it expands to make more than a quart of ice.

Suppose that freezing water is prevented from expanding? Suppose that freezing water is in a space where there is no room to expand? In that case, the water produces a tremendous **force** as it turns to ice. The force made as water turns to ice is great enough to split rock!

When rain falls on rock, water may run into cracks in the rock. If the water freezes (perhaps during a cold night), it expands in the crack.

We know that, as water freezes, the expansion can produce a great force. The force of freezing water widens the crack a little. ●

This can happen again and again. It rains. Water flows into a crack in the rock. It gets cold and the water freezes. As it freezes, the water expands. The crack in the rock gets wider. At last the crack gets so wide that the rock splits. The piece that breaks off may tumble down the side of the mountain. Along with other pieces it makes a heap at the bottom. These pieces may be split again and again into still smaller pieces. They may be carried away by running water.

Look at this close view of the heap of rocks piled against the side of a mountain. ■ You can see that there are large pieces of rock and smaller pieces. Most of them have sharp edges. Freezing water helped make this heap. The next time it rains, water rushing down the mountain will carry smaller pieces away. These bits of rock will become soil.

Soil may be carried away by running water. Small rocks may be carried away by running water. Big rocks, even mountains of rock, may be broken down into small pieces by freezing water. Then they may be carried away by water, too.

BEFORE YOU GO ON
Study these statements and choose the correct responses. Your study will help fix in your mind the main concept of this section.

1. Freezing water
   a. expands   b. contracts

2. When water gets into a crack in a rock and freezes, the rock may
   a. split   b. pull together

3. As a mountain breaks down, its rock
   a. is carried away   b. piles up on the top

USING WHAT YOU KNOW
1. A bottle of milk is left outside on a very cold winter day. The milk freezes. The bottle breaks. Can you tell why?

2. This sign is seen by the side of a road cut through rock. What could cause the rock to fall?

ON YOUR OWN   Does the temperature sometimes go below freezing, where you live? See if you can find some places where freezing water has done its work on sidewalks.

3. The Heat of the Sun

Have you ever put your bare foot on a sidewalk on a hot day and found that the sidewalk was hot enough to burn your foot? The sidewalk has been heated by the Sun, of course. Bare rock can get very hot when heated by the Sun, too. This helps to break down rock. Let us see how.

You may have done this investigation. ■ If you have, you will remember that when the bottle is heated, the balloon gets bigger. The balloon gets bigger because the air in the bottle expands when heated. Then, as the air in the bottle cools, the air gets smaller, or contracts. As the air contracts, the balloon gets smaller again. Air expands when heated and contracts when cooled.

Here is another example. Heat makes the liquid inside a thermometer rise. This happens because the liquid expands as it is heated and rises inside the tube. When the thermometer is put in a cooler place, the liquid becomes cooler and contracts. As the liquid contracts, it takes up less room and goes down in the tube.

Most substances expand when heated and contract when cooled. This is also true of rocks. Rocks expand when heated and contract when cooled. This helps to break down rocks. Let us see how.

During the day, the rays of the Sun heat a rock. The outside of the rock becomes hot, but the inside

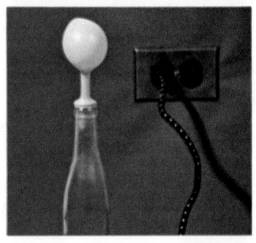

does not become hot. As this happens, the outside of the rock expands. At night, the rock becomes cool again, and its outside contracts. Day after day, and night after night, the surface of the rock expands and contracts, expands and contracts. The surface of the rock peels off. The surface that has been heated and cooled breaks off in layers. This happens especially when there is a large difference between the heating and cooling.

In time, the peeled-off pieces of rock break down still more. They may be carried away by running water. The heat of the Sun then goes to work on the fresh surface of rock that has been laid bare.

So the Sun breaks down rocks by making them expand. It does more, however. The Sun helps plants to break down rocks. How can a little plant break down hard rock? Try the investigations on the next two pages to find out. INVESTIGATE

The Force of a Plant

Seeds swell as they soak up water. They expand, and they can push with great force against anything that holds them in. Then, as seeds grow, they develop stems and roots. The roots push out against anything holding them in.

Imagine some seeds falling into a small crack in a rock. In the crack there is a bit of soil. Perhaps wind carried the soil there or water brought it there. When rain comes, the seeds take in water. They expand. They sprout. Their roots dig into the bit of soil and spread into every part of the crack, pushing against the rock. As the plant grows, it forces the crack just a little wider. ■ In the winter, water may freeze in the crack and expand and widen the crack still more.

You see, then, that plants can break down rock, helped by the Sun from which they get the energy to grow. The Sun's heat can break down rock by making it expand again and again. Water can break down rock as it seeps into cracks and then freezes and expands.

Water, Sun, plants, all working together, can break down mountains. It takes time, of course. It takes millions of years. But this breaking down of rock and carrying away of soil has been going on for a good many millions of years, and it will continue.

AN INVESTIGATION into the Force of Sprouting Seeds

Needed: a small bottle and a cork to fit it, enough bean seeds to fill the bottle, a paper bag

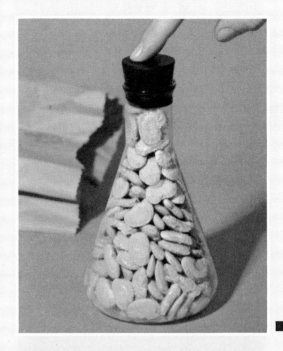

Fill the bottle up to the neck with the dry bean seeds. Add enough water to just cover the beans. Put the cork in. ■

Put the bottle in the paper bag to keep the seeds dark. Seeds sprout best in the dark. In about 3 or 4 days the seeds will have sprouted.

What happens to cork and bottle?

Here is what happened in one trial.●

Now try the investigation on the next page.

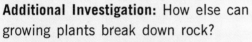

Additional Investigation: How else can growing plants break down rock?

Lichens are plants that grow on rock in flat, brown or gray patches. Look for rocks on which lichens are growing. Remove part of the lichens, and examine the rock underneath. How is this rock different from rock where the lichens are not growing? How do you explain what you observe?

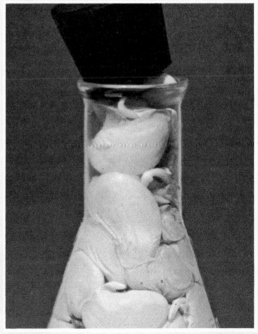

AN INVESTIGATION into What Happens When Plants Grow

Needed: two pieces of glass, a piece of blotter, rubber bands, a pan, lima-bean seeds that have soaked overnight

Put the blotter on a piece of glass. Put some seeds on the blotter. ■

   Place the second piece of glass on top of the seeds. Put rubber bands around the two pieces of glass to hold them together. ●

   Lay the glass sandwich in a pan with just enough water to reach the blotter. As the roots grow, do they pry the pieces of glass apart? Here is what happened in one trial. ▲ What would happen if the roots grew into a crack in rock?

Additional Investigation: Can other growing parts of the bean plants push the pieces of glass apart?

■

●

▲

BEFORE YOU GO ON Study these statements and choose the correct responses. Your study will help fix in your mind the main concept of this section.

1. Generally, when substances are heated, they
   a. expand   b. contract

2. The surface of a rock when heated and cooled may
   a. peel off   b. be built up

3. Roots of a plant may cause a rock to
   a. disappear   b. break apart

USING WHAT YOU KNOW 1. How does expanding and contracting help break down a rock?

2. When rock is heated, it expands. When air is heated, it expands. Do you know a substance that expands when it is cooled?

3. There are air spaces between lengths of steel rails. What would happen if there were no spaces between these lengths of rail? Why?

Collect some evidence with a camera to show what plants can do to rock. Write on the back of each picture where and when you took it, and what you think the plant is doing to the rock.

4. Building Up the Land

We have seen how ice and heat and plants break up rock and how

running water carries away soil and small rocks. We have seen how the land is being torn down and moved away. Little by little, the mountains are being worn down, and the soil is being carried away by running water.

What happens to this soil and rock? We can find out if we look once more at our model river, in the investigation on page 221. The model river, you remember, carried sand down to the bottom of the sand hill. In fact, the little river made a small pile of the sand that it had carried along at the bottom of the hill. ■ The water made a model lake there, where it dropped the sand.

Why did the model river drop the sand it was carrying at the bottom of the hill? Try the investigation on the opposite page. It will help you to answer this question and perhaps others. **INVESTIGATE**

Down in the Valley

The model river dropped its load of sand where it did for a reason.

AN INVESTIGATION
into Moving Water

Needed: a large jar, some coarse sand with small pebbles in it, a spoon, water

Put about an inch of sand in the jar. Then add water until the jar is about three-fourths full. ■

When the sand has settled to the bottom of the jar, begin to stir the water gently around the jar with the spoon. Do not let the spoon touch the sand. Keep the spoon near the surface of the water.● Observe how much sand the water is carrying along.

Now stir the water faster. Does the load it can carry change? Stir still faster. What happens to the amount of material carried as the water moves faster? ▲

Take the spoon out of the water quickly. The whirling water begins to slow down. As it slows down, what happens to the load it is carrying? ◆

Does the same thing happen each time you repeat your investigation?

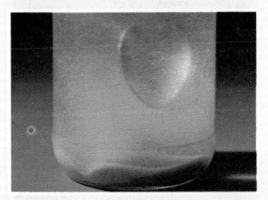

Additional Investigation: As the water slows down, do the heavier particles or the lighter ones drop out first?

235

The running water slowed down there. When the running water slowed down, it could not carry as much sand as it had been carrying. So the water dropped most of its load of sand at the foot of the little hill, where the water slowed down. The faster water flows, the more material it can move along. The slower it flows, the less it can carry.

Why did the model river slow down just at that place? It was because the water was not running downhill any longer, of course.

When the water in the model river suddenly slowed down, it dropped a lot of the sand it was carrying along.

Does the same thing happen in a real river? See for yourself. Here is a photograph of a place where a stream enters a valley. The fast-running water suddenly slows down. As you see, it drops soil and rocks that it was carrying.

The bits of soil, rocks, leaves, and other materials that a river carries and drops are called **sediment.** Some of the soil and rocks taken from the mountains is carried into valleys and dropped as sediment. The running water may drop layer upon layer of sediment. Thus *land is built up in the valleys,* even as it is torn down in the mountains.

If you live near mountains or if you have visited them in the winter, you know that they may be covered with a deep blanket of snow. Ice is also at work breaking up the rocks. Spring comes and with it warm rains that melt the snow and ice. Many streams rush down the mountainsides carrying large amounts of soil and bits of rock. The streams join to make a river that flows through a valley.

A river flowing through a valley becomes swollen with rain. It is carrying much sediment and moving swiftly. ● The river rises and overflows its banks, flooding the valley. ▲ Where the valley is flooded, the water now moves *slowly*. The water drops much of its load of sediment. When the flood waters go, that sediment remains in the valley. ◆ Thus the land in the valley is built up.

Down to the Sea

Imagine rain falling on hills and mountains and running into small streams. The small streams run into larger streams, the larger streams tumble into rivers. Small rivers join to make big rivers, such as the Ohio, the Mississippi, the Columbia, and the Delaware. After a time, some of the sediment may come to rest at the bottom of the sea.

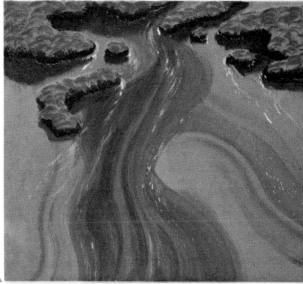

237

The place where a river pours its water into the sea is called the **mouth** of the river. At the mouth of a river, the water usually slows down as it meets the sea. As the river water slows down, it drops some of the sediment it is carrying, of course. As a river drops sediment at its mouth, it builds up land there. Here is the mouth of the Mississippi River. ■ Can you see where the river has dropped sediment? Each year the Mississippi River becomes a little longer, as more land is built up at its mouth.

You might think now that when the Mississippi has reached its mouth, it has dropped all its soil and rock. But it hasn't. The river still has sediment in its water. This sediment is carried out to sea and dropped on the sea bottom. The land at the bottom of the sea is being built up by every river that carries soil and rock down to the sea.

The land is being torn down and carried away in some places. In other places the land is being built up, built up with the soil and rock that was torn down.

A handful of soil now on a hill in Ohio may travel to the bottom of the sea in a year or two. Another handful of soil on a mountain in Oregon may travel to the Pacific Ocean in the same time.

Study these statements and choose the correct responses. Your study will help fix in your mind the main concept of this section.

1. Whenever land is being broken down, land is being built up
   a. in the same place   b. in another place

2. Land is built up at the mouth of a river as soil is
   a. dropped   b. carried away

3. Bits of rock and soil from a mountain
   a. may be found at the bottom of the sea
   b. can never be found in the sea

USING WHAT YOU KNOW

1. Is there any evidence in this picture to show that more water once flowed in this stream?

2. The Nile River in Egypt floods its valley every year. After the flood waters leave, farmers begin their planting. Why is the soil in the valley richer after a flood?

3. Do you agree or disagree? Tell why.

a. As land is worn down in one place, it is built up in another place.

b. The slower a stream flows, the more soil and rock it can carry along.

ON YOUR OWN Look for evidence after a heavy rain to show that when running water slows down, it drops part of what it is carrying. Photograph the evidence or make a drawing of it to show to your class.

5. Holding Land and Water

Water can carry soil away.

We need soil. We must have soil to live. Are there ways to keep water from carrying soil away? Are there ways to hold soil?

Here is a geranium plant that is growing well. Hold the plant and tap the pot on the side to loosen the soil. ■ Lift the plant out of the pot.● The soil comes out as well. What is holding the soil together?

Pull up a few weeds and look at their roots. What comes up with the roots? Try to take all the soil off the roots. It is not easy. The weed roots hold soil.

Roots hold soil. Where there are no plants and the soil is bare, water can carry the soil away. But if plants are growing in the soil, their roots hold on to the soil. Water cannot wash the soil away easily. This is one reason why it is important to have forests. Trees have many roots, and their roots hold much soil.

Trees help to hold soil in another way. The leaves of a tree can act as a **cover.** A cover is a kind of shelter that protects soil from being washed away.

Cover in a Forest

If you have ever been under a tree when it started to rain, you

have probably heard the sound of raindrops hitting the leaves. It is an important sound. It means that the leaves are helping to hold the soil. Raindrops that hit leaves first do not hit the soil hard. They drip down onto the soil. When there are no leaves, the raindrops can hammer at the soil, break it up, and wash some of it away. Leaves on the trees act as cover. In the fall, when leaves drop to the ground, they again act as cover. The carpet of leaves keeps the soil from being washed away.

Have you ever been in a pine forest? The trees are so close together that you are sheltered from a gentle rain for a while. Then the rain begins to drip gently to the carpet of pine needles under your feet. This deep cover several inches thick soaks up the heaviest rains. An oak or maple forest usually has shrubs, ferns, and other small plants growing among the trees. These, too, break the force of rains and their dead leaves add to the cover of the forest floor.

As you can see, leaves help hold soil. Besides leaves, there is one plant that is especially important for holding soil in place. This important plant is grass. But first see how a cover protects the soil. Try the investigation on the next page. INVESTIGATE

AN INVESTIGATION into How Leaves Help to Hold Soil

Needed: some soil or sand, four or five leaf-sized pieces of paper, a sprinkling can, a brick or wood block, an empty aquarium or large pan

Make a flat pile of sand on the brick or block in the aquarium or pan. Lay paper "leaves" on the sand. ■

Sprinkle the sand with water. The higher the can is above the sand, the harder the "rain" will fall. ●

What happens to the sand under the cover of the "leaves"? What happens to the sand that was not under cover?

Here is what happened in one trial. ▲

Additional Investigation: Place some pennies on a flat pile of sand. Predict what will happen if you sprinkle the sand with water. Test your prediction.

Saving Our Soil

Soil on a bare hillside is easily washed away by rain. In time, the running water cuts deep into the soil. It makes deep slits and ditches called gullies. When there is a heavy rain, streams of water flow down the gullies and make them deeper and wider. In time, so much soil may be washed away that the hillside may look like this. ■

But if a bare hillside is planted with grass, the story will be different. Grass is a cover for soil. The roots of the grass hold soil and keep it from being washed away. Gullies do not get a chance to start. Something else happens as well where grass grows. The rain soaks into the soil. Water that soaks into the soil does not run off to do damage else-where. The grass roots hold the soil, and the soil holds the water.

If a gully has become deep, planting grass may not be enough. Dams may have to be built across the gully to break the force of running water and to catch the soil it may be carrying. Vines, shrubs, and seedling trees can be planted along the sides. In a few years, the cover they provide will slow down the flow of water. The soil can be built up again so that it will be useful.

There are many ways of holding the soil we need.

Study these statements and choose the correct responses. Your study will help fix in your mind the main concept of this section.

1. To hold soil, we should
   a. cut down trees   b. plant trees

2. To hold soil, we should
   a. permit leaves to remain on the forest floor
   b. remove leaves from the forest floor

3. To hold soil, we should
   a. permit plant roots to remain in the ground
   b. dig up the plant roots

1. Do you agree with these statements? Tell why.
   a. We need soil.
   b. Roots break up soil, causing it to be washed away.
   c. Leaves make a good cover.

2. The kudzu vine has large leaves and grows very quickly. Can you think of a good use for such a plant?

3. A farmer has a field on the side of a hill, which he is going to plow. If he wants to keep his soil from being washed away, should he plow up and down the hillside? across the hillside? What is your reason?

Photograph some examples of soil being washed away. Decide what you think might be done to stop it, in each case.

6. The Rising Mountains

From a distance, mountains seem unchanging and able to last forever. When we look closer, however, we see cracks in the rock, pieces of rock that have broken off, and streams carrying soil and rock away. We know that the mountains are always changing. Water, ice, the heat of the Sun, plants, and other things are wearing down the mountains.

As water runs down hills and mountains, it picks up soil and rock and carries them along. It drops them in the valleys and plains, at the mouths of rivers, and on the sea bottom. Thus, in one place land is being worn down. In another place land is being built up. ■

All along our shores there are rivers running into the sea. All along our shores these rivers are carrying soil down to the sea. Millions and millions of tons of sediment are laid on the sea bottom every year by rivers. A tremendous weight of soil and rock is built up on the sea bottom along the shore. This weight of sediment along the shores gets so great, we think, that it makes a change in the Earth. To understand what this change is, and how it happens, you should first know something about the inside of the Earth.

Do you think that the Earth is solid rock all the way through?

The melted rock below the Earth's crust can flow, like toothpaste, if it is squeezed. If you squeeze a partly filled tube of toothpaste in one place, what happens? The toothpaste flows to another part of the tube. If you press down on one part of the tube with a finger, what happens? The tube rises in another place as the toothpaste flows there.

Strangely enough, the Earth may be behaving like a tube of toothpaste. If the Earth is pressed down in one place, it may rise in another place. And hot melted rock within the Earth may flow to another place as the Earth is pressed down.

What could press down on the Earth's crust in one place?

Up Go Mountains

Along the seashore, rivers are dumping sediment into the sea. (Sediment includes all the bits and pieces of soil, rocks, leaves, and other materials that a river picks up.) This is going on now. It has been going on for millions of years. On the bottom of the sea, near the shore, the load of sediment gets heavier and heavier. The growing weight of sediment presses down on the Earth's crust harder and harder. The growing weight of sediment presses on the

Inside the Earth

Scientists have found that our Earth is not cold, hard rock all the way through. Not at all. Only the **crust** of the Earth, the outside, is solid.

Below this solid crust of the Earth there is hot, melted rock. Every now and then some of this hot rock is pushed out through the solid crust, rather like toothpaste being squeezed out of a tube. When this happens, a **volcano** is made.

melted rock inside the Earth, harder and harder.

Think of this, too. As the weight of sediment on the sea bottom is getting heavier, the mountains are getting lighter. The mountains are being worn down, remember.

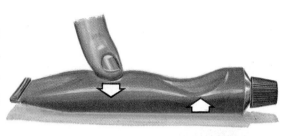

The sediment brought from the mountains presses down in one place. The Earth's crust may rise in another place. It may rise under the worn-down mountains. It may rise along the seashore, near where the sediment is pushing down. Where the crust rises, it may make mountains. ▲

It may be, too, that heat inside the Earth helps raise mountains. As sediment falls on the sea bottom, it makes a kind of blanket. The part of the Earth under that blanket becomes warmer. The heat may cause the rock to expand and to push up the crust.

This is one explanation of how the crust of the Earth is pushed up. There are other explanations which you will study as you go on in science.

We do know that there are places where the Earth's crust is rising. We do know that there are mountains that are rising, ever so slowly. Some scientists believe that this rising is

▲

explained by the weight of the soil and rock dumped into the sea by rivers. Others believe that the heat trapped under the blanket of soil helps raise these mountains, even though very slowly. If you look at a map of the United States, you can notice something interesting about our mountain ranges. They run in the same direction as our coasts. This is what they might be expected to do, if they were somehow connected with the seashore.

Land is worn down. Land is built up. Mountains rise again. The Earth is never still. It changes all the time. It changes every second, every year, as it has been changing for many millions of years. It will keep on changing.

BEFORE YOU GO ON Study these statements and choose the correct responses. Your study will help fix in your mind the main concept of this section.

1. The inside of the Earth is
   a. hot   b. cold

2. Heat inside the Earth may
   a. press mountains down   b. help raise mountains

3. The pressure of great weights of sediment may
   a. help raise mountains   b. press mountains down

USING WHAT YOU KNOW 1. How can heat under the crust of the Earth help to lift mountains?

2. As old mountains are being worn down, new mountains are rising up. Do you think this is a cycle? Why?

ON YOUR OWN Clams live in the sea. Yet clam shells millions of years old are found in rock on top of a mountain. How do you explain this?

7. The Main Concept: The Earth Is Changing

The Earth is changing, changing all the time. Often we do not notice it, because many of the changes happen so slowly. Yet they are happening. Rocks are breaking down. Water seeps into cracks at the top of mountains. The weather gets cold and the water changes to ice. As it does so, it pushes against the sides of the cracks. The rock splits and breaks up. In summer, roots of plants work into other tiny cracks in the rocks and widen them still more. Then, in winter, ice works again to widen the cracks. Melting snows and spring rains move rocks and soil (and bits of dead plants and animals) down the mountain into the valley.

These bits of rock and parts of plants and animals make more soil. More plants can grow in this soil. As they die, they add substances to the soil. So more soil is always being made.

As plants and animals grow and die, the soil is being changed, too. The dead animals and plants are putting useful substances back into the soil. They are making the soil good for more plants to grow in, providing food for animals.

Running water is picking up soil in one place and dropping it in another place. Plains and valleys are being built up with soil in which plants can grow. Plants are useful in saving soil, too. If water runs too fast, the good soil is carried away and only poor soil is left. Plants do not grow well in poor soil. If there are enough plants—trees, bushes, and grasses—water does not run off so fast. Plants keep water from carrying off soil. This means that the substances plants need remain in the soil.

Streams carrying soil are flowing into rivers. Rivers are emptying into seas and dropping rock and soil and other materials along the seacoast. The weight of this sediment on the sea bottom is getting heavier and pressing down harder. Under the sediment at the bottom of the sea, under the Earth's crust, melted rock is moving and pushing against the crust. As the Earth's crust is pressed down in one place, it is pushed up in another—and mountains are slowly rising.

Yet even as they are rising, the mountains are being worn down, and land is being built up somewhere else. It happens over and over again. It is happening now. The surface of the Earth is always changing and will always keep on changing.

Fixing the Main Concepts

TESTING
YOURSELF Study the statements below and choose the correct responses. They will help fix in mind the main concepts.

1. Small pieces of rock are found broken off a big rock. They may have been broken off by
   - a. heat
   - b. wind

2. Rivers that move slowly are not likely to carry
   - a. large stones
   - b. small particles

3. When muddy water slows down, soil is
   - a. dropped
   - b. picked up

4. Grass is important because it can
   - a. break up soil
   - b. hold soil

5. In a forest, the soil is protected against hard rain by
   - a. leaves on the ground
   - b. open spaces

6. The heat of the Sun acts mainly to
   - a. build up mountains
   - b. break down mountains

7. The heat below the surface of the Earth acts mainly to
   - a. raise mountains
   - b. break down mountains

8. The rock of a mountain is broken down by the
   - a. leaves of plants
   - b. roots of plants

9. A river may get longer by dropping sediment
   - a. anywhere
   - b. at its mouth

10. The surface of the Earth is
    - a. not changing
    - b. changing

FOR YOUR READING

1. *The Colorado: River of Mystery*, by Mary and Conrad Buff, published by The Ward Ritchie Press, Los Angeles, 1968. How does a river change the face of the Earth as it flows toward the sea over hundreds of years? Find out from this interesting account of the Colorado River.

2. *The Earth's Story*, by Gerald Ames, published by the Creative Educational Society, Mankato, Minnesota, 1967. This book tells the Earth's story in beautiful photographs.

3. *Where Does Your Garden Grow?* by Augusta Goldin, published by Thomas Y. Crowell, New York, 1967. What makes some soil good and other soil poor for plants to grow in? Which plants will grow in which kinds of soil? These are only some of the things you can find out from this helpful book about soil.

GOING FURTHER

An Investigation

Different kinds of soil have different kinds of fungi living in them. To study these different fungi, collect some soil samples. You can keep the different soils in clean pint jars. Be sure the jars are dry. Fill each jar to the brim with soil. Cover the jars with wax paper fastened with a rubber band. Some of the kinds of soil that you might collect are: garden soil; sandy soil; clay soil; soil from a forest; soil from the side of a pond; soil from about 1 foot beneath the surface, if possible; soil that is usually moist; soil that is usually dry. Do not forget to label each jar.

Place two tablespoonfuls of a sample of soil in a plastic bag. Add one-fourth of a slice of bread. Close the bag and label it. The molds will begin to grow. Do this for each of your samples.

Which soil produces the richest fungus life? You can observe the speed with which molds grow and the number of different kinds of mold. CAUTION: *Once molds begin to grow, do not open the bags.* Remember that molds reproduce by spores. The spores can spread from an opened bag and spoil food.

Keep a record of your observations. Drawings and photographs will help. In a few weeks you may have an idea of which soil is richest in fungus life. (How do your results compare with someone else's?)

How will you know that the molds did not come from the bread? Can you plan your investigation to make fairly certain that the molds came from the soil?

Beginning a Hobby

To learn about soil, use it, dig it, care for it. A farmer's life depends on keeping his soil in good condition. Your life does too, for you depend on the farmer.

One way to learn about soil is to start a garden. Your garden might be in a few flowerpots or a window box. Perhaps you know someone who can help you begin. You may want to start with a book, perhaps this one.

First Book of Gardening, by Virginia Kirkus, published by Franklin Watts, New York, 1956. This book is for beginners, and it should give you a good start.

You don't need much land to begin a garden. All you need is a sunny spot, perhaps 6 feet long by 6 feet wide. The soil should be at least 12 inches deep. Of course the soil should have humus in it and not be too sandy. Suppose you decide to grow beans and tomatoes. You can grow 6 tomato plants and 2 or 3 rows of bean plants. When they are ready to pick, your tomatoes and beans will be fresh, and they will taste fresh—not like canned or frozen food. Instead of beans and tomatoes, you may prefer to grow peas and radishes.

You can grow flowers in a small garden: daffodils, zinnias, snapdragons, asters, and many other colorful and beautiful kinds. Catalogs from seed and plant breeders can help you make a choice.

Why is growing plants fun? Why do people like this hobby? For one thing, they like being outdoors as they turn over the soil and weed the garden so that the plants can grow well. For another, they like watching how what they do helps the vegetables grow better, or the flowering plants grow larger with more blossoms. They like seeing how fertilizers and watering and regular weeding help the plants grow.

Gardening is a hobby that can grow from year to year. But you can start with a few flowers or vegetables, depending on how much land you have and how much time you want to spend. In time, you may become an expert.

UNIT EIGHT

THE VOYAGE OF HALLEY'S COMET

The year is 1910. People look with wonder at the strange object in the night sky. It is Halley's comet, moving across the background of stars. In a few weeks it vanishes. But people who are there remember it for the rest of their lives.

If you had been there in 1910, you would not have forgotten it either. You won't when you see the comet in 1986.

What makes us think that this comet will appear again? What makes us think that it will appear at a certain time?

The answer begins with a look at the Moon.

1. The Voyage of the Moon

Everyone has noticed that the Moon always seems to be changing shape. The changes happen over and over again, so often that we do not usually pay much attention to them. If you could observe the Moon night after night for a few weeks, you would see that its shape changes like this. See the pictures marked at the left. ■ These changes are repeated over and over, in a cycle. It takes the Moon about 28 days to go through one cycle; that is, it takes this time for these changes.

We do not pay much attention to this cycle. It just happens, and goes on happening, whether we pay attention to it or not. But let us ask ourselves *why* the Moon's shape seems to change. These changes tell us some interesting things about the Moon, the Earth, the Sun, and other bodies in space as well. What do these changes in the Moon's shape mean? See for yourself by doing the investigation opposite. `INVESTIGATE`

The Light of the Moon

Look at the changing shape of the ball in the investigation. Look at the changing shape of the Moon. The shapes are alike, aren't they?

AN INVESTIGATION into Seeing a Lighted Ball

Needed: a flashlight, a ball, a dark room

The darker the room is, the better. Let someone hold the flashlight so that you can stand some distance away from it but in its light. Hold the ball in your hand, like this. ■ Now turn slowly so that the ball moves in a circle around you. (Raise the ball to keep it out of your shadow, if necessary.)

What happens to the shape of the lighted part of the ball?

Now hold the ball in each of these positions. ● Draw the shape of the lighted part of the ball, as *you* see it, in each position.

Why does the shape of the lighted part change?

Additional Investigation: Look at the Moon at the same time each evening for a few weeks. On the evening that you start, what shape is the Moon?

Draw this shape in your notebook. How many days go by before you see the Moon that shape again?

How do you explain why it took that long for the Moon to appear that shape again?

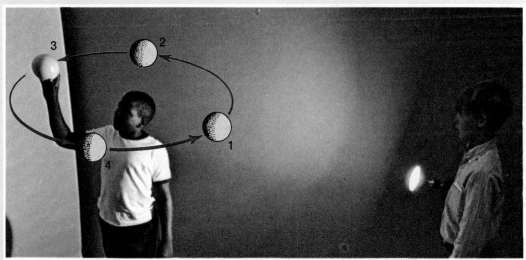

The shape of the ball does not really change. It remains a ball. What *does* change is the shape of the lighted part.

Why does the shape of the lighted part of the ball change? *The shape changes because the ball is moving.* As the ball moves around you, the shape of the lighted part changes.

Why does the shape of the lighted part of the Moon change? The shape changes because the Moon is moving. The Moon is moving around you, much as the ball moved around you in the investigation.

Let us take a look from a distance at our Earth and its Moon. Imagine that we are in a spacecraft about 100,000 miles away from the Earth. We look back at the Earth and its Moon. What do we see?

We see that the Earth and the Moon are lit by the far-off Sun. As we watch, we see the Moon slowly moving around the Earth. It takes about 28 days to make one trip around the Earth. It follows the same path around the Earth each time. We call this path in space an **orbit.** The Moon is in an orbit around the Earth. ■

We see, too, how the shape of the lighted part of the Moon changes. When the Moon is off to one side of the Earth, it seems to be a **half moon** to someone on the Earth. When the Moon is on the far side of the Earth from the Sun, it seems a **full moon** to someone on the Earth. And the **new moon** is on the same side of the Earth as the Sun.

Let us get down to Earth again. There is something else we can observe about the Moon from the Earth. However, as we see the changing shape of the Moon in the sky, from night to night, we now know what that changing shape ■

means. The changing shape of the Moon means that the Moon is moving.

The Face of the Moon

Look again at the photographs of the Moon, on page 256, but this time look closely at the Moon's face.

Does the face of the Moon change as the Moon is following its orbit around the Earth? It does not, as you can see. The face of the Moon does not change, because the Moon always has the same side toward us. As the Moon moves in an orbit around the Earth, it keeps the same side facing the Earth.

Ever since men have known this, they have wondered what the other side of the Moon was like. Was it very different from the side we see? When a satellite traveled around the Moon and took photographs of the other side, we discovered that the other side of the Moon seems to be much the same as the side we see.

You may know that scientists of several countries are interested in what the Moon is like. These rocks are rocks on the Moon's surface. ● Some of them were brought back by astronauts from the United States who landed right on the Moon. By studying such rocks carefully, scientists are learning

more about the Moon's history.

It takes the work of many scientists and others to land a spacecraft on the Moon. As you know, the Moon is always moving in an orbit around the Earth, moving silently through space. Scientists had to be sure the Moon would be in just the right position before they sent the spacecraft onward to the Moon.

What does the moving Moon have to do with a **comet,** a heavenly body with a tail of glowing matter? What has the moving Moon to do with a comet that is supposed to appear in 1986, Halley's comet?

Let us return to Halley's comet and see.

Study these statements and choose the correct responses. Your study will help fix in your mind the main concept of this section.

1. The Moon has a cycle which takes about
   a. 28 days   b. 14 days

2. In its cycle the lighted part of the Moon which we see
   a. changes its shape
   b. does not change its shape

3. The path of the Moon around the Earth is called
   a. a shape   b. an orbit

4. The changing shape of the Moon reminds us that the Moon is
   a. far away   b. moving

1. Where is the Moon in its orbit when we see a half moon?

2. The shape of the Moon itself does not change. The shape of the lighted part of the Moon changes. Does the shape of the lighted part of the Earth ever change? How do you know?

Are you reading about man's attempts to reach the Moon? Keep a scrapbook of newspaper and magazine clippings on "Project Moon."

2. The Voyage of a Comet

People used to be afraid of comets.

A comet, you see, was something that did not seem to belong in the sky. The stars seemed to be always in their places, fixed and unmoving. The planets and the Moon all moved, to be sure. Yet they moved in regular ways and in the same orbits all the time. You could count on their regular behavior.

Then suddenly a comet might appear. A comet looked like nothing else in the sky. Sometimes it was strangely bright. It moved across the sky and in a few weeks disappeared. Where did a comet come from? Where did it go? No one knew. It frightened people. They felt that a comet was a sign that something bad was going to happen: war, disease, floods, or who knew what?■

Comets used to be feared. A man named Halley changed that.

Halley's Discovery

Edmund Halley was an English scientist who lived over 200 years ago.● He was interested in many things, but he was especially interested in comets. Where did comets come from, and where did they go?

Halley wanted to know. He studied the observations of comets, which other scientists had made. The orbit of a comet was a very difficult problem in mathematics. He could not figure it out. Neither could other scientists who tackled the problem.

However, Halley had a friend named Isaac Newton, who was a brilliant mathematician. Could Newton possibly figure out what the orbit of a comet would be like?

Yes, he could. In fact, he had already worked out that problem, Newton thought. But he could not find the papers on which he had done it. He would work it out again. Presently Newton showed Halley what shape the orbit of a comet would have.

Now Halley set to work. He figured out the orbits of some of the comets that had been observed by scientists. He made a surprising discovery. The comets that had appeared in the years 1531, 1607, and 1682 had the same orbit.

It seemed very strange to Halley. Three different comets following the same orbit, the same path in space? The more Halley thought about it, the more he thought that there had not been three different comets, as people thought. He decided that they had simply seen the same comet three times. *The comet had gone away and had come back again.*

It was an astonishing idea! Halley felt certain enough to make a prediction of what would happen in the future. He predicted that this comet would appear in the year 1758.

The same comet had appeared, if Halley was right, in 1531, in 1607, and in 1682. Its appearances had been 75 to 76 years apart, then. Halley predicted that the comet would return 76 years after its last appearance. It would appear in 1758.

Halley's Comet

Remember, no one had ever predicted the appearance of a comet before. Remember that comets were thought of as strange and wild and frightening things. Moreover, there were 53 years to go before Halley's prediction could be tested.

In 1758 the comet appeared in the sky. Halley had been right. Halley did not see it, for he had died some years before. Ever since then that comet has been called Halley's comet, in his honor. Since then, Halley's comet has returned at the predicted times. It will return, we can predict, around the year 1986.

We do not fear comets any more. Halley's discovery made comets a part of the sky, like the stars and planets and Moon. What is the orbit of Halley's comet? Where does it come from, and where does it go? Make the model on the opposite page. It will give you an idea of the voyage of a comet. INVESTIGATE

MAKING A MODEL: The Orbit of a Comet

Needed: about 34 feet of heavy string, chalk, masking tape, a yardstick, and a large, clear floor or playground

First draw a scale model of part of the solar system. Mark the Sun in the center. Draw circles for the orbits of these planets: Earth, Mars, Jupiter, Saturn, Uranus, Neptune. To draw each circle, use the radius marked on that planet's orbit in the picture. ■

With the string, make a loop that is 16 feet 2 inches long. Tape the loop to the floor at the Sun and, stretched out, at 15 feet 8 inches from the Sun.

Hold the chalk inside and against the loop, as shown. Keeping the string taut, move the chalk along the loop. It will trace an orbit like that of Halley's comet, swinging around the Sun and out into space beyond Neptune's orbit, and back.

Additional Investigation: Try placing a model of the Earth and of Halley's comet at different positions on their orbits. At which positions might Halley's comet be seen from Earth?

tape
Sun
Earth $5\frac{5}{8}$ in.
Mars $8\frac{3}{8}$ in.
Jupiter 2 ft. 6 in.
15 feet 8 inches
Saturn 4 ft. 6 in.
Uranus 9 ft. 0 in.
tape
Pluto
Neptune 14 ft. 0 in.

Study these statements and choose the correct responses. Your study will help fix in your mind the main concept of this section.

1. Edmund Halley had the help of the mathematician
   a. Charles Darwin   b. Isaac Newton

2. Like the Moon and Earth, comets have
   a. an orbit   b. a spherical shape

3. Three comets which appeared about 76 years apart had the same orbit. Halley said they must be
   a. the same comet   b. different comets

4. Scientists can predict when some comets will appear because they can calculate some comets'
   a. shapes   b. orbits

Why are people no longer afraid of comets?

3. Newton and the Moon

Halley figured out the orbits of other comets besides the one that bears his name. You may remember, however, that he first had to ask his friend Newton what the orbit of a comet was like. Halley could not solve the problem of the orbit, nor could any other scientist except Newton. He had already solved the problem, but he could not find his papers, you recall. He had to work out the answer again.

What did Newton tell Halley? Newton told Halley that the orbit of a comet had the shape of an **ellipse** (ih·LIPS). An ellipse is the shape of a flattened circle. Here are a few ellipses. ■ The orbit you made in the investigation on page 263 is an ellipse.

How did it happen that Newton was able to answer Halley's questions? How did Newton know that the orbit of a comet is an ellipse? He knew because he was a careful observer and thinker.

The Pull of the Earth

Throw a ball straight up. It slows down, it stops for a moment, then it starts back to the ground. It seems to be *pulled* to the surface of the Earth. Anything that you throw into the air will act in the same way. It will always go up, stop, and then fall back to the ground.

Let go of a pencil, a coin, a rock, this book. They fall to the ground. They seem to be pulled to the surface of the Earth. Hold this book in your hand. You can feel the pull of the Earth on the book.

It doesn't matter where you are. If you are at the top of a tall building or a cliff, any object you drop will always fall to the ground.

The Earth has a pull on every object on the Earth. We call this pull **gravitation** (grav·ih·TAY·sh'n). It is the pull of gravitation that makes objects fall to the ground. It is the pull of gravitation that holds objects to the ground, and holds you, too. When you have to lift an object, the pull you lift against is the pull of gravitation. Gravitation pulls everything on Earth. In fact, gravitation pulls on things near the Earth, too, as you know. Balls and birds, kites and airplanes, are pulled down by gravitation.

When you look at the Moon calmly sailing through the night sky, you might not think of gravitation. Isaac Newton did. Newton had an idea that the pull of gravitation reached out from the Earth to the Moon. He showed that the Moon is being pulled to the Earth by gravitation, just like other objects.

Balls and birds, kites and airplanes, are pulled down by gravitation. So is the Moon, said Newton. This poses another question, however.

If the Moon is being pulled to the Earth by gravitation, why doesn't the Moon fall to the Earth?

You can get a clue to the answer by trying the investigation on the opposite page. **INVESTIGATE**

Pulling on the Moon

The Moon is moving. It would move away from the Earth, except for the pull of gravitation.

A ball rolling along a level floor moves straight ahead. To make the ball go in a curve, it must be *pulled* around. It is the pull of the thread that makes the moving ball go in a curve around your hand. It is the

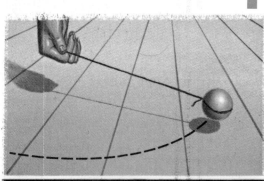

pull of gravitation that makes the moving Moon go in a curve around the Earth. ■

What happens if you let go of the thread tied to the moving ball? The ball rolls away. What would happen to the Moon if the pull of gravitation stopped? The Moon would sail away from the Earth, into space.

The Moon is pulled by the Earth's gravitation. However, the Moon does not fall to the Earth because the Moon is moving. It would move away from the Earth, except that the pull of gravitation keeps it curving around the Earth.

It was Isaac Newton who worked out these ideas about the Moon and the Earth and gravitation.

Newton did something more. He figured out, by mathematics, what sort of orbit the Moon has. He found that the orbit of the Moon around the Earth is an ellipse. In fact, he found that the orbit of any object moving around another and pulled by gravitation is an ellipse. The orbit of a comet is an ellipse. That was what Isaac Newton told Edmund Halley.

Halley was able to understand what Newton was talking about. The concept of gravitation helped him to predict that the comet he was studying would return at the time it did.

AN INVESTIGATION
into a Moving Ball

Needed: a tennis ball, about 4 feet of strong thread, a smooth, level floor

Tie one end of the thread to the tennis ball. ■

Hold the other end of the thread in your hand, and ask someone to give the ball a gentle push along the floor. *Keep the thread slack.* Let your hand move along to let the ball move freely. Does the ball roll in a straight line or in a curve?

Here is what happened in one trial. ●

Now hold the end of the thread to one place on the floor. *Keep the thread taut.* ▲ Ask someone to push the ball again. Does the ball roll in a straight line or in a curve?

Here is what happened in one trial. ◆

What do you feel in the string as the ball rolls in a curve?

To make the moving ball go in a curve, what is needed?

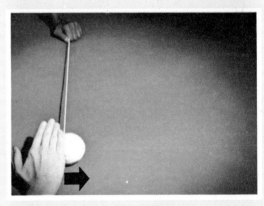

Additional Investigation: Try using a thread that is half as long. What happens to the curve? What happens to the pull? Is more or less pull needed to make a sharper curve?

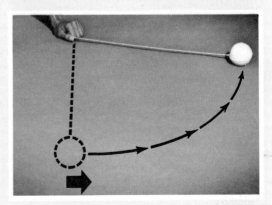

You see, now, one reason why Isaac Newton is a very famous scientist. He dared to think that gravitation was more than just a pull on things on the Earth, pulling down apples and dogs and houses and people. He dared to think that gravitation reaches out beyond the Earth, to the Moon. It pulls between the planets and the Sun, and even between the stars. It pulls between all bodies traveling in space.

BEFORE YOU GO ON Study these statements and choose the correct responses. Your study will help fix in your mind the main concept of this section.

1. When you lift an object, you pull against the pull of the
   a. Earth   b. Moon

2. The Moon would move away from the Earth if it were not for
   a. gravitation   b. its round shape

3. A pull is needed to make a moving ball go in a
   a. straight line   b. curve

4. The pull of gravitation acts
   a. only on objects on the Earth
   b. on all objects

USING WHAT YOU KNOW 1. A spacecraft gets very near the Moon. What might happen to the spacecraft?

2. A satellite is shot into space and goes into orbit around the Sun. What will be the shape of its orbit? Why?

ON YOUR OWN Every now and then maps in the newspaper picture the orbit of a satellite. Check to see whether the orbit is an ellipse or not. Will there ever be an exception? Find one.

4. Comets and Some Other Space Travelers

Right now, as you read this, Halley's comet is heading toward the Sun, swinging in toward us from far out in the solar system, from beyond the orbit of the planet Neptune. As it curves around the Sun, we shall see it for a few weeks. In 1986, when Halley's comet is near the Earth, it will probably look something like this. ■ Then back out to the edge of the solar system the comet goes.

What is it that we see when we look at a comet? What is a comet made of?

A Ball of Ice

What are comets made of? This question has puzzled astronomers for many years. It still puzzles them. They are still not quite sure what comets are made of. They think, however, that a comet's *head*, the round, bright part, is a mixture of ice and bits of rock and dust. The ice has come from frozen gases. The head of a comet is like a huge, dirty snowball, someone has said.

The *tail* of a comet is a stream of very thin gases. The tail usually grows from the head as the comet gets nearer the Sun, and becomes longer and longer. However, it always

■

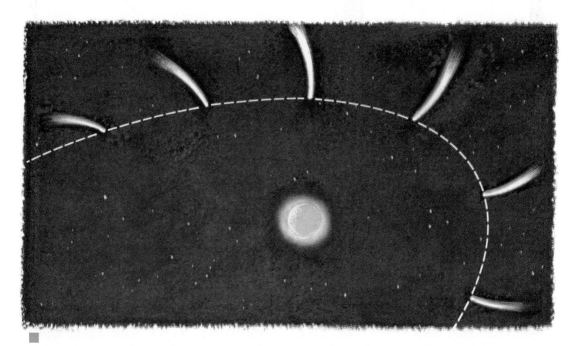

streams away from the Sun, as the comet swings around the Sun. ■ The comet then becomes brighter, too. A comet has no light of its own. It is lit by the Sun's light, like the Moon.

Astronomers suspect that millions of icy comets are swinging through space around the solar system. Every so often one of these balls of ice and rock swings in toward the Sun, and comes close to the Earth.

As a comet nears the Sun, some of its ice may turn to gas. In time, after several trips around the Sun, a comet may disappear. Halley's comet's last appearance, in 1910, was not as spectacular as the one before. It may be shrinking, but it still should make a good show in 1986.

When the ice of a comet turns to gas, what happens to the rocks and dust that were in the ice? These bits may become another kind of space traveler, a kind that we see much more often than comets. Some of these rocks may become "shooting stars," as people call them.

Not all scientists agree that "shooting stars" come from comets. Some scientists think the evidence is not clear. Investigations are being carried on now to get more evidence.

Since a "shooting star" is not a star at all, that is not a good name for it. It is called a **meteor** (MEE·tee·or). If you look for meteors, you may find them. Try the investigation on the opposite page. INVESTIGATE

AN INVESTIGATION into Meteors

Needed: a clear view of the night sky with no Moon, away from lights; two or three friends

Spring	Summer	Fall	Winter
April 21	July 29	October 22	January 3
May 5	August 12	November 17	
		December 12	

Meteors may be seen at any time of night, but usually more may be seen in the later hours. Your friends and you might watch different parts of the sky, and call out when you see the flash of a "shooting star." ■

At certain times of the year, as the Earth travels its orbit in space, we see more meteors than at other times. Look for such meteor "showers" during the weeks of the dates given in the table.

Observe these things about meteors:
—Are they equally bright?
—Are they the same color?
—Do they come from the same direction?
—Do they last the same time?

Additional Investigation: How many meteors do you see each hour? Compare your count with that of your friends, and of scientists. ■

A Streak of Light

When you have looked up into a night sky, you may have seen a sudden streak of light shooting across the sky for a short distance. ■ Just as suddenly as the streak appears, it vanishes. It is a meteor, a lump of rock speeding through space, which suddenly becomes white-hot and gives off light. Just as suddenly the light vanishes. What has happened?

Lumps of rock from the head of a shrinking comet may be of all sizes. Some may be pebbles, some huge boulders, some like dust. Imagine a large lump of rock speeding through space. The rock comes near the Earth. It is pulled toward the Earth by the Earth's gravitation. The lump of rock, speeding 20 to 40 miles each second, enters the Earth's **atmosphere** far above the Earth.

The atmosphere far above the Earth contains very little air. Even so, the rock is now speeding through some air. When one surface moves across another, they rub against each other. We say there is **friction** between them. Because of the friction, heat arises.

Press your hands together hard. Rub them against each other. Do your hands get hot because of the friction? When a meteor speeds through air,

there is also friction. The meteor gets very hot—hot enough to glow. This is the light we see when we see a meteor. The light goes out when the meteor has burned up.

Sometimes a meteor does not completely burn up. It plunges through the atmosphere and hits the Earth. It is then called a **meteorite.** When a meteorite crashes into the Earth, it may make a large hole, like this one. ● Here is a meteorite that was dug out of the hole it made in the Earth. ▲ There are billions of such objects scattered throughout the space of the solar system.

Study these statements and choose the correct responses. Your study will help fix in your mind the main concept of this section.

1. A mixture of ice, bits of rock, and dust is in a comet's
   a. tail   b. head

2. A comet has
   a. no light of its own   b. its own light

3. As it goes around the Sun, a comet may
   a. lose some of its substances
   b. gain some substances

4. Meteorites are found
   a. in space   b. on the Earth

5. A meteor may come from
   a. the Sun   b. a comet

How could rocks in space be dangerous to space travelers?

5. When Scientists Predict

Halley's comet loops around the Sun about every 76 years. Scientists can predict the comet's coming and going. There are other comets, too, whose appearances can be predicted.

When will there be a full moon in the night sky again? The date can be predicted. The Moon moves around the Earth in an orbit. Scientists can predict where in that orbit the Moon will be at any time. The planets move in orbits around the Sun. Their positions can be predicted. When the Earth will speed through a cloud of rocks in space can even be predicted. Because scientists can predict, we know when to watch for meteor showers.

We are so used to such predictions that we think nothing of them. Let us, however, think about them. Why are scientists able to predict?

Knowing What Makes It Work

Ask a young child what happens if he lets go of a ball in his hand.  He will tell you that the ball will fall, of course. (He may think that you are rather stupid to ask, too.) He makes a prediction about the ball. He knows that the ball has always behaved that way in the past. He expects that it will go on behaving that way. He predicts that it will.

This is one way of predicting, certainly. You have, however, been studying a better way in this unit.

Why are astronomers able to predict that Halley's comet will appear again in 1986? Not just because that comet has appeared again about every 76 years for at least 2,000 years that we know of. Scientists predict the return of that comet because they understand what makes it return.

What makes Halley's comet come back? The shape of its orbit, which is an ellipse. What shapes the orbit of the comet? The pull of gravitation. There is not any sign that the pull of gravitation is going to stop working. Gravitation shapes the path of the comet. So long as this is so, that path may be predicted.

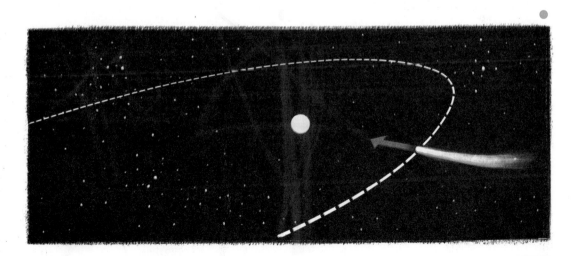

Gravitation shapes the path of the Moon around the Earth. Gravitation shapes the path of the Earth around the Sun. Gravitation shapes the paths of the planets around the Sun, and of the stars in the universe. So far as we know, gravitation is not changing. So we do not expect changes in the orbits of the Moon, the Earth, and the planets. Thus their orbits can be predicted. We understand something about what makes them work.

If *you* were asked what would happen to a ball when you let go of it, you would give the same answer as a young child. You would make the same prediction. Your prediction, however, would be more scientific. You know something about what makes the ball work that way.

The Tardy Comet

Halley's comet turns up about every 76 years, on the average. Yet Halley's comet does not always appear again in just 76 years. Sometimes it appears in as few as $73\frac{1}{2}$ years, sometimes in as many as $78\frac{1}{2}$ years. Halley's comet probably will appear again more than 76 years from its appearance in 1910.

Sometimes Halley's comet passes near the planet Jupiter. ■ Jupiter, like every other body, has a pull of gravitation. When Halley's comet comes close enough to Jupiter, the comet may be held back a little because of this gravitation. As a result, the comet may take a little longer to reach the Earth. Or sometimes the comet may be pulled forward a little, and reach the Earth a little sooner.

Even so, scientists can calculate when the orbit of the comet will pass close to Jupiter. Gravitation is at work. They can calculate what effect Jupiter's pull will have. They can still predict the arrival of Halley's comet accurately.

There is more to making predictions than this, of course. However, science is a way of finding out how the world works. Scientists can make predictions when they understand how a thing works.

So can you.

BEFORE YOU GO ON

1. Why can scientists predict the positions of the Moon and Earth?

2. Why can scientists predict the time of the return of Halley's comet?

3. How can scientists predict when Halley's comet will be late?

ON YOUR OWN

List some things that you can predict because you know how they work. Here are two predictions to start with: a ball will fall to the ground; a saucer of water will evaporate.

6. The Main Concept: Regular Change

An astronaut may travel in orbit around the Earth in about 88 minutes.

The Moon travels in orbit around the Earth in about 28 days.

The Earth travels in orbit around the Sun in about 365 days.

Halley's comet travels its orbit, around the Sun and beyond Neptune and back, in about 76 years.

Earth, Moon, and comet change their positions every moment. They are always moving. They are never still. And yet, we know that these movements can be foretold. Scientists are able to predict where these restless bodies will be in the future. Scientists can predict because they understand the forces that are at work on these bodies. They know what forces shape the orbits of the Moon and the Earth. They know the forces that shape the long ellipse of Halley's comet.

They know that while comets, planets, Earth, and Moon are always changing position, the force of gravitation does not change. That is, the effect of gravitation on comets, planets, Earth, Moon, or any body, does not change. The effect of gravitation remains unchanged.

So in the midst of movement and change, in the midst of what seems at first disorder, we have been able to find a hidden order. We have found that change can be regular.

Fixing the Main Concepts

Study the statements below and choose the correct responses. Your study will help fix in your mind the main concepts of this unit.

1. The Earth's orbit
   a. cannot be predicted   b. can be predicted

2. The orbit of a space satellite
   a. can be predicted   b. cannot be predicted

3. Halley's comet has
   a. a predictable orbit
   b. an orbit which is not predictable

4. Meteors
   a. always hit the Earth
   b. do not always hit the Earth

5. The orbit of a planet is
   a. a circle   b. an ellipse

6. An orbit is shaped by
   a. the pull of gravitation
   b. the prediction of scientists

7. Halley made his discovery
   a. without using the work of other scientists
   b. by using the work of other scientists

8. Scientists think that a comet's head may partly be made of
   a. liquid water   b. ice

9. Newton told his friend Halley that the orbit of a comet was
   a. impossible to calculate   b. an ellipse

10. When Halley's comet gets near the planet Jupiter, it is attracted to Jupiter by the force of

      a. friction   b. gravitation

FOR YOUR READING

1. *A Book of Mars for You,* by Franklyn M. Branley, published by Thomas Y. Crowell, New York, 1968. This easy-to-read book takes you on a make-believe trip to the planet Mars in a spacecraft. You discover whether it is possible to live on Mars.

2. *Exploring and Understanding Rockets and Satellites,* by David Posin, published by Benefic Press, Westchester, New York, 1967. You will find out from this book how a spacecraft is able to leave the Earth and go into orbit around it. You may also want to carry out some of the investigations in the book.

3. *Shooting Stars,* by Herbert S. Zim, published by William Morrow and Company, New York, 1958. Here is a good book about meteors. The book tells you how meteors arise, what they are made of, and where they appear.

4. *Worlds in the Sky,* by Carroll L. Fenton and Mildred A. Fenton, published by the John Day Company, New York, 1963. This fine introduction to astronomy tells you many things about the earth, the solar system, and the stars.

GOING FURTHER

You were born into the Space Age. Perhaps you will discover a new comet. It has been done by young people not much older than you.

Why not investigate how comets have been discovered?

A New View of Change

The mountains look as if they could stand forever, unchanging. Yet we know that they cannot, for they are changing. Heat and cold, water and wind are slowly breaking them down.

A little water runs into a crack in a rock. ■ The water freezes in the crack. As the water freezes, it expands. The crack widens. During the day, the heat of the Sun makes the rock expand. In the cold of the night, the rock contracts. Cracks appear, and widen. Wind and rain wear away the rock surface and carry off bits of rock.

Slowly, slowly, the mountains are being broken down. Streams and rivers pick up the tiny bits and carry them away. When the running water slows down, it drops the bits in valleys and lakes and oceans. And so, slowly, the land is built up again. Along the seacoasts the rivers deposit millions upon millions of tons of this material on the sea bottom. As this great weight presses down in one place on the crust of the Earth, the crust may rise slowly in another place. For under the Earth's crust is a doughy layer of hot rock that can

■

flow under great pressure. This is one way in which new mountains may be made. So, over millions of years, mountains are being worn down in one place, and raised up in another place.

The concept is plain: the Earth is changing.

Living Things Change

Nor is the Earth the only thing that is changing.

Here is a plant that once grew on the Earth. ● It no longer grows anywhere on the Earth. It has disappeared, and other different kinds of plants have taken its place.

You recall that many kinds of animals that once lived on the Earth are no longer found. These ancient plants and animals gave rise to other plants and animals which are alive now. Slowly, and little by little, living things on the Earth have changed. Slowly, plants and animals on the Earth are changing now.

The concept is plain: living things are changing.

The Earth changes its place in space. It is rotating. It is revolving in an orbit around a star, the Sun, along with other planets. The group of stars to which the Sun belongs is moving, as well, through space.

●

Changes You Can See

Look at a burning log, a melting piece of ice, an evaporating puddle of water. All around you, matter changes. Rub your hands together. Your hands get warm. You have changed the energy of your moving hands into heat energy. Energy changes. Look at a planted seed. It grows, and changes. A young puppy grows and changes. Salmon, ducks, geraniums, flies change.

Look at a picture of yourself taken only a year ago. You have changed. You are changing now. Life changes. The Earth changes. The universe changes.

Understanding Change

Changes are all around us. We study these changes. We learn more and more about them. As we do this, something happens. We begin to understand why changes happen. And we can predict changes. We can say what will happen, before it happens.

We can predict where the Earth will be in its orbit ten years from today. We can predict what will happen to planted seeds. We can predict the arrival of a comet in the night sky. We can predict some of the changes that will happen to the surface of the Earth. We can even predict some of the changes that will happen to living things.

We still have a great deal—an enormous amount—to find out and learn. But with what knowledge we have, we can begin to predict a few of the changes that are always going on around us and happening to us. We can begin to predict because we are beginning to understand what makes the changes happen. Thus we can learn to live in the midst of change.

Remember, too, that man is more than a living thing to which changes happen. A seed cannot plan to make changes. It cannot plan to alter the world it lives in, if that world is not a good one for it. A seed cannot do anything to bring the water it needs to where it lies, for instance. A seed cannot make deliberate changes in its environment. But man can make changes. Man can plan to change the changing world in which he lives. Man can use his mind to understand the changing world, and use the knowledge he obtains to make the changing world a better place to live in.

To do this, man needs not just knowledge and understanding, but wisdom. For the changes that man plans now shape the future for man to come. ●

PROBING WITH A MICROSCOPE

A drop of pond water is a world in itself. It is a world of such strange animals and plants that you will find it hard to leave once you enter it.

How can you enter this world? How can you explore it and probe it? You can use a microscope and simple equipment, such as jars, and medicine droppers, and slides.

First, however, you must catch some of these living things. Then you must feed them and shelter them, so that you can observe them as you want to. When you stop to think that these living things are so small that you can't see them with your eye alone, catching and feeding and housing them may sound difficult. It isn't hard at all.

Collecting Invisible Living Things

Take a field trip with a grown-up. Bring along five jars with caps, about this size. ■ Look for a small pond

■

or a stream that flows slowly. ■ Even a small ditch with water in it may do. Look for one in which water plants are growing.

Plan how you can collect the pond water safely. (Talk this over carefully in class.) Fill each jar about three-quarters full of the water from the pond. If you can, get some mud or water from the side as well. ● If plants growing near the surface

of the water are within reach, add a bit of plant to each jar. ▲ However, it is the pond water that you want. The mud and plants are not as important, so don't try to gather them if they are not within easy reach. Cap the jars tightly.

Bring the jars of water home, or back to the classroom, and let them stand for twenty-four hours. Let them stand in a cool place—avoid heat if you can. And don't put the jars in bright sunlight. Medium light, not very bright, is best. This will give things a chance to settle down.

Don't keep the jars tightly capped. Unscrew the caps and set them on top of the jars, loosely. In this way they can let air in, yet keep dust and dirt out of the water.

Growing Invisible Living Things

The pond water in the jars contains tiny living things. It contains tiny animals, called protozoans, that are made up of only one cell. It contains tiny green plants called algae. If you looked at a drop of this water through a microscope, however, you might not find one of these protozoans or algae. You could examine drop after drop of water until a protozoan or an alga appeared, but you might have to examine quite a lot of drops. Fortunately there is a better way. It is to get the protozoans and the algae to reproduce. If conditions are right, they will reproduce in large numbers. Then there will be so many of them that almost any drop of the water will have protozoans and algae in it.

If these living things are to grow and to make more of their kind, they must have food, of course. Here are some good ways to feed them.

Boil an egg until it is hard—about twenty minutes. Take a piece of the yolk about the size of a pea. Crumble the piece of yolk between your fingers, letting the crumbs drop into one of your jars of pond water. Label that jar "Egg yolk." ■

Get a little rice. Drop about five grains of the rice into another jar. Label it "Rice."

Put five grains of wheat into one more jar. Label it so that you know what food is being used in this jar.

Put no food into the two jars that are left. Let those jars stay as they were when you collected them, so far as food goes. ●

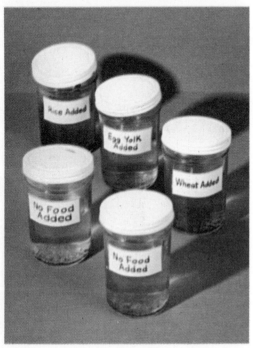

Return all five jars to the place where they are not too warm and do not get too much light during the day. Observe them carefully, day by day. Within a week or two (if your pond water had any protozoans in it to begin with) the jars will swarm with tiny specks that you can see moving about. These specks will be protozoans and other animals.

Which jars do you suppose will have the most tiny animals? Which kind of food will produce the most protozoans—egg yolk, rice, or wheat?

The egg yolk and the grains of rice and wheat are not food for the protozoans, by the way. The egg yolk, the rice, and the wheat furnish food for bacteria in the water. Bacteria are very tiny plants, each made up of a single cell. (They are not green, even though they are plants.) As the bacteria feed on the egg yolk, it decays —so these bacteria are called decay bacteria. Some decay bacteria are illustrated on page 162. The decay bacteria and small protozoans are food for large protozoans.

Now, with your own supply of growing and reproducing protozoans and algae, you can study the kinds of living things in a drop of water.

Using a Microscope

Here are some things you need, as well as a microscope, for observing life in a drop of water: slides, cover slips, a medicine dropper. ▲

Let's examine a microscope, first. ◆ The upper lens, the one you look through, is called the eyepiece. The lower lenses are called objectives. There is a number on the top of the eyepiece of this microscope: "10×." Each of the objective lenses is marked with a number also. One lens is marked "10" and the other lens is marked "40." These numbers indicate the magnifying power of these lenses. The eyepiece magnifies ten times. The objective lenses magnify ten times

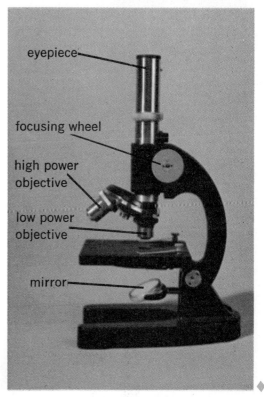

eyepiece

focusing wheel

high power objective

low power objective

mirror

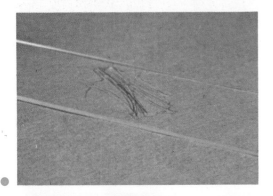

and forty times. How much does this microscope magnify? Multiply the number on the eyepiece by the number on the objective being used. For the low-power objective, marked 10, this is 10 × 10, or 100. Using low power, the microscope magnifies 100 times. An object placed under the low power lens looks 100 times as big as it actually is. Multiply the number on the high power objective by the number on the eyepiece: 10 × 40 is 400. The high-power objective magnifies 400 times.

The wheel at the side of the microscope is for focusing. When the wheel is turned, the distance between the objective lens and the object being observed is changed. The mirror is for reflecting light onto the object being examined.

Perhaps the easiest way to begin using the microscope is by looking at one of your own hairs. Follow these steps.

—Take up a little clean water in the medicine dropper. Put a small drop on a slide. ■

—Put a piece or two of hair from your head in the drop. ●

—Touch a cover slip to the edge of the drop of water. ▲

—Gently lower the cover slip onto the drop. It will flatten the hairs a little, making them easier to examine, and prevent the drop from evaporating quickly. ♦

Now the hairs are mounted on a slide and ready to be examined.

—Swing the low-power lens into place under the eyepiece. It will click into place.

—Put your eye to the eyepiece. Turn the mirror toward a window or a light so that light is reflected into the microscope. You will see a bright circle of light in the eyepiece.

—Take your eye from the eyepiece. Put the slide under the clips on the microscope stage so that it is held firmly. Place the slide so that the hair is in the light from the mirror.

—Turn the focusing wheel so that the low-power objective moves slowly down toward the slide. Stop when you see the lens is about an eighth of an inch from the slide.★

—Now put your eye to the eyepiece and turn the focusing wheel the other way so that the lens moves up, away from the slide. *Be sure to turn the wheel so that the lens moves away from the slide.* If you turn the wheel the wrong way, you may run the objective into the slide, break the cover slip and the slide—and scratch the lens. Turn the wheel until the hair is in focus, as sharp and clear as possible.

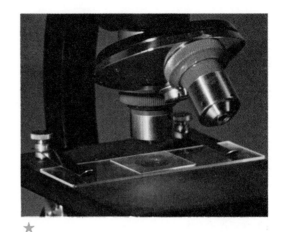

★

—Try moving the slide around with your fingers carefully, while looking through the eyepiece, so that other parts of the drop can be seen. ◈

—To look at the hair through the high-power objective, swing the high-power objective around until it clicks into place under the eyepiece. It will be very nearly in focus. Move the focusing wheel very carefully, for the high-power objective is very close to the cover slip and slide!

◈

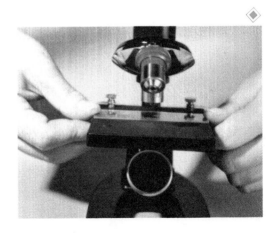

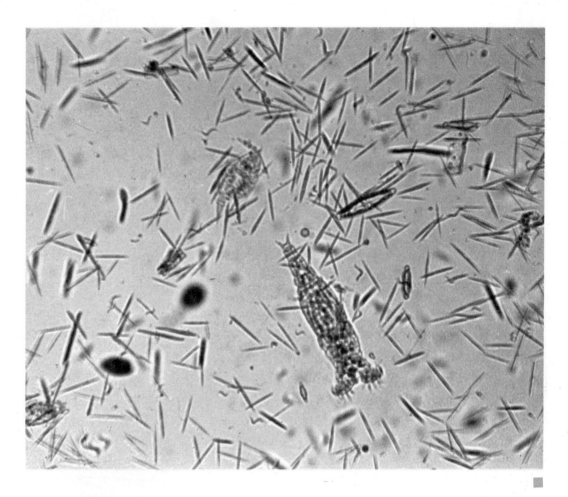

—To remove the slide, swing back to low power again, then move the slide off the stage. The slide and the cover slip may be rinsed with water, and dried with tissue paper.

Probing a Drop of Water

Now you can use the microscope to explore the world of living things in a drop of water. With a clean medicine dropper, take a little water from one of your jars of growing and re-

producing living things. Take water from a place where the moving specks are thickest.

Place a drop of this water on a clean slide. Cover the drop with a cover slip. Place the slide on the microscope and examine the drop under the low power. (Always use the low-power lens first.) Move the slide slowly and carefully with your fingers. With a little practice you may be able to follow a moving living thing by shifting the slide. Switch to the high power for closer examination.

Here is the sort of scene you might see at first. ■ It contains many different living things, both plants and animals. To help you identify some of them, here are some pictures and names. It is a good idea to know names if you want to talk about what you have seen, or if you want to get more information about some of the strange animals you may encounter. ●

There may be green growths on the side or bottom of your jars. There may be some green living things in the mud scraped up from the pond. Examine them under the microscope. You may find some algae, simple green plants, like these. ▲

Explore drops of water from different parts of your jar, and from different jars. When you have made the acquaintance of some of the animals

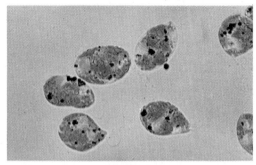

Euglena

Rotifer

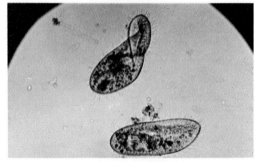

Paramecium

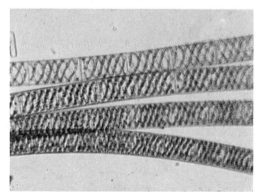

Spirogyra

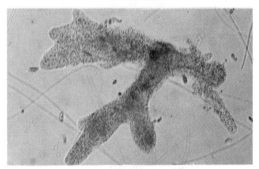

Ameba

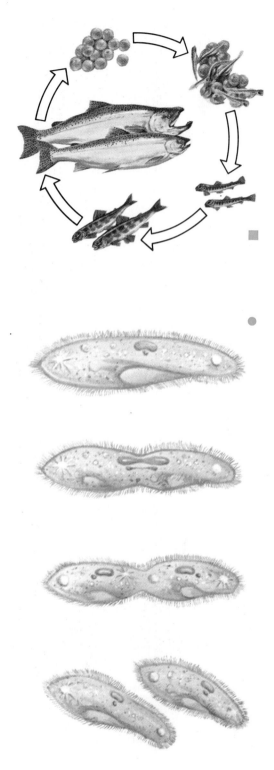

and plants that live in a drop of water, you may want to know more about how they live. Try some of the investigations that follow.

INVESTIGATIONS

A Protozoan's Life Cycle

You know that many events take place in what we call a cycle—a certain order that is repeated over and over.

The salmon, for example, have a life cycle that begins with eggs. The eggs grow (some of them) to be young salmon. The young salmon (some of them) grow to be adults. The adult salmon produce eggs—and the life cycle starts over. ■

Every living thing has a life cycle. What is the life cycle of a protozoan like, then?

To investigate this, a good thriving collection of protozoans is needed, a *culture* of protozoans, as scientists say. Such a culture is a kind of tiny pond, isn't it? It is a kind of pond you can observe closely, and when you wish.

Use the microscope to find in a culture some animals that seem to be dividing in two, like this one.● When you find one or more dividing protozoans on a slide, seal the edges of the cover slip to the slide with petroleum jelly.▲ This will prevent the drop of water from evaporating. Drying out will kill the protozoans quickly. By sealing the cover slip you can observe a dividing animal for some time. Try to observe a dividing animal (which is called a parent) until it separates into two animals (called daughters). Are the daughters like the parent? Are they about the same size as the parent?

Most of the tiny animals in your cultures reproduce by dividing in two. This dividing in two is known as fission. But some of the animals in the culture reproduce in other ways than by fission. Page 298 suggests some of these ways.

There are many different animals and plants in your cultures. In some ways you could compare the population in one of your culture jars with the population of plants and animals in a forest. For instance, the population of animals in a forest depends on plants for food. (Even the animals that eat other animals depend on plants, in the end.) Your population of protozoans depends on plants, too. For example, paramecia feed on bacteria. Bacteria are plants. Other protozoans feed on paramecia, as you can see here. ♦

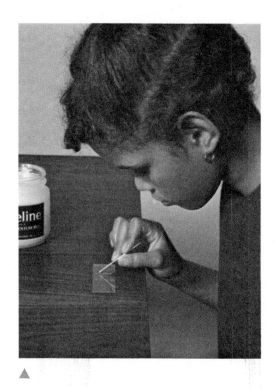

▲

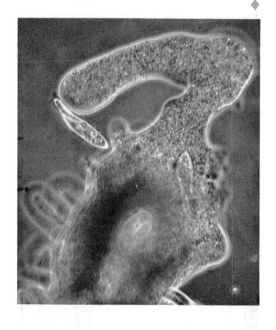

♦

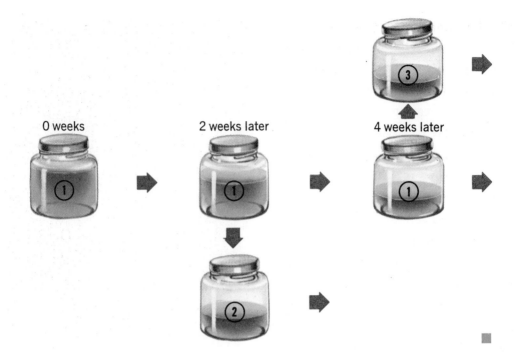

The animals in a forest depend on light and air. So do the protozoans in your cultures.

Sometimes in a forest one kind of animal will reproduce in extraordinary numbers. Sometimes it may be the rabbits, sometimes the deer. On the whole, though, the population in a forest stays in a kind of balance. You might have a hard time observing this in a forest, but it is not hard to study the population in your cultures.

Does the population of protozoans in your cultures remain about the same, or does it change? Every day examine drops of a culture from different parts of a jar. Take water carefully from the sides, bottom, and top of the jar with the dropper. Try not to disturb the culture while doing this.

Keep a record every day of your observations. See what answers you can find to questions like these:

—Which animals in the culture seem to be greatest in number? How long do they remain so?

—Is there any change in the kind of animal that is greatest in number as the culture gets older?

—After about four weeks, how does the population of the culture differ from the population at the beginning?

Of course, whatever you observe will be happening in only one culture.

Will the same sort of thing happen to the animals in another culture? What is your guess? To find out, start some more cultures.

Starting New Cultures

Collect a jar of pond water again, about three-fourths full. Crumble a little hard-boiled egg yolk into it, as you did before. Label it "Culture 1." From this culture you can start two more cultures that will give you a clearer idea of the growth cycles. Start Culture 2 from Culture 1 after Culture 1 has been growing for about two weeks. Start Culture 3 from Culture 1 after Culture 1 has been growing for about a month. ■

To start Cultures 2 and 3 you must of course prepare the environment in which the animals and plants can live. Put water into a jar until it is about half full. Water from the tap will do. Crumble a pea-size bit of hard-boiled egg yolk into the jar. Let the jar stand for three days. During this time bacteria will feed on the egg yolk and develop. You should do this, then, three days before it is time to start a new culture from Culture 1.

About two weeks after Culture 1 was started, stir the culture thoroughly. Then pour about one third of Culture 1 into the new jar, where

it can develop by itself. Label the new jar "Culture 2." ●

Two weeks later, stir Culture 1 thoroughly again and pour about one half of it into a prepared new jar. Label this "Culture 3."

You can observe how each culture develops by examining drops of water from each one under the microscope.

What differences can you observe between the populations of the three cultures?

Do the populations in the cultures go through the same sort of cycle, no matter when they were started? Or do the different cultures have different cycles?

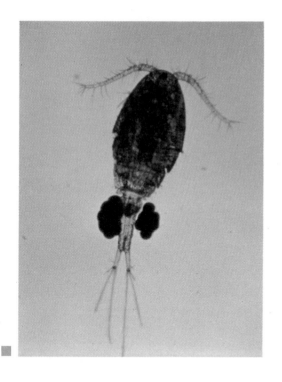

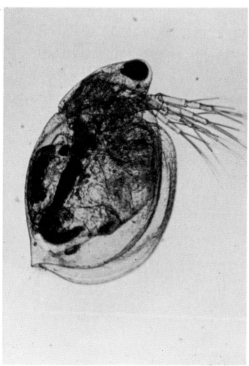

As you observe what happens in the three cultures, you will probably think of some interesting questions of your own. Why not investigate them?

More Investigations to Try

Some of these animals in your pond cultures reproduce by dividing in two, by fission, that is. Others reproduce by means of eggs.

If your pond culture has Cyclops or Daphnia in it, examine them under the low power of the microscope. Can you see eggs on each side of the Cyclops' body? ■ Can you see eggs, or unborn young, inside the Daphnia? ●

See if you can observe how long it takes a Daphnia or a Cyclops to reproduce. One way to do this is to take a fresh supply of water swarming with bacteria that you have prepared as food for your pond culture. Put some in a very small bottle. Capture, in a drop of water, a Cyclops or a Daphnia which is carrying eggs. Add this drop to the water in the small bottle. How long is it before young Daphnia or Cyclops appear in the water?

You may have to do this several times because all eggs do not develop.

How do the microscopic animals in your pond water culture behave? You can observe this, too. Try this investigation. Pour a thick culture of Euglena into a clean test tube until the tube is about three-quarters full. Stand the tube in a rack or a glass tumbler.

Don't disturb the tube for about ten minutes. At the end of that time the tube may look something like this. ▲

What has happened in this tube? Most of the animals have gathered at the top of the tube.

Why?

Is it because there is more air at the top of the tube?

Is it because there is more light at the top?

Is it because the animals move against the force of gravitation?

What can you do to find out?

There are many other kinds of behavior that you can observe and study in a drop of water. Here are a few.

How do different animals in the pond water culture catch their food?

How do different animals move about?

How do different animals avoid their enemies?

If you continue to watch the world in a drop of water under the microscope, you will surely think of questions of your own that you want an-

swered. And you will think of ways to investigate your questions. You may find yourself wanting to read what other people have found out about something that interests you. You may find yourself wanting to talk with other people about something you have discovered, or something you want to try. Reading about things that interest them, finding out what other people have done, talking over how investigations might be done, swapping knowledge and ideas— these are things that scientists do when they are on the trail of something interesting.

▲

KEY CONCEPT WORDS:
A BEGINNING VOCABULARY
FOR SCIENCE

To record what they have learned from their investigations, scientists use words that have the same meaning to every other scientist. That is, scientists try to use words accurately. You are building up a vocabulary of key concept words of science during this year, which you will of course want to use correctly. The first time a word is used with a special meaning for scientific communication, it is in boldface type in your textbook. In this vocabulary of key concept words, a page reference is given to refer to if you need more information or examples of the meaning than is given here. In other words, the definition given here is a short, first definition that needs filling out. The complete meaning of the word cannot be given here as you need more work in science for full understanding. A few terms you probably know from earlier work in science do not have a page reference; you already know how to use these words in their correct meaning. The words may be used a number of times in this textbook; the Index will help you see how these words are used accurately throughout your work in science.

Words that may be difficult to pronounce are respelled in parentheses after the word. Each syllable is pronounced just as it is spelled. The syllable that has the accent is in capital letters.

absorb (ab.ZORB), to stop the movement of the molecules in a sound wave instead of bouncing them back, 24; to take up a substance or energy, 32

adapted, fitted by its structure for life in a certain environment, 165

algae (AL.jee), tiny green plants, generally single-celled, 179

atmosphere (AT.mus.feer), the layer of gases around the Earth; the air, 272

atom, a building block of elements; atoms combine chemically to build molecules, 105

bacteria (bak.TEER.ee.uh), tiny plants that can be seen only with a strong microscope; they have only a single cell and no green coloring matter, 90

behavior (beh·HAYV·yur), the way a living thing responds to its environment, 204

carbohydrate (KAHR·boh·hy·drayt), a compound of carbon, hydrogen, and oxygen; it has twice as many hydrogen atoms as oxygen atoms. Any sugar or starch made by green plants, 149

cell, the smallest living unit of any living thing, 154

cell division, the dividing of a cell to make two new cells that are alike, 155

chemical change, any change in which a substance is broken down into other substances, or is built up from other substances. In chemical change, atoms of a substance (or substances) become joined in a different way, 44

chemical reaction (KEM·ih·kul ree·AK·sh'n), chemical change; term usually used by scientists for any chemical change they explain exactly, 122

chlorophyll (KLOR·uh·fil), a substance in the cells of green plants which enables them to make sugars, 160

combine (kum·BYN), to join with, as iron and oxygen molecules join to form iron oxide, 105

comet (KOM·it), a body in space traveling in a long orbit around the Sun; it has a head and tail of matter that glow when the comet is near the Sun, 259

compound, a substance made up of atoms of two or more different elements, 108

condense, to change from a gas to a liquid. In **condensation,** loss of heat energy makes invisible gas molecules move closer together and form visible liquid, 68

confirm, to test a possible explanation to find if it is correct, as to test a theory, 115

constellation (KON·stel·lay·sh'n), a group of stars having a fixed pattern in a part of the sky.

contract (kon·TRAKT), to move closer together and take up less space. In **contraction,** molecules move closer together, 71. Muscle cells also contract.

convex lens, a lens that is thicker at the center than at the edges; it focuses light, 40

cover (kuv·OR), plants, leaves, grass, or other things that keep soil from being washed away by rain, 240

crust, the solid outside layer of the Earth, 246

current (KUR·ent), a flowing of a substance in a certain direction, as ocean currents or air currents, 80

decay, to become broken down into simpler substances. Wood and other substances decay and become humus, 161

diffused (dih·FYOOZD), reflected in all directions; spread out, 33

displace, to take the place of. In the **displacement method** of collecting a gas, gas forced through water in a bottle takes the place of the water, 100

dissolve (dih·ZOLV), to mix completely in a liquid, as salt or oxygen in water, 83

echo (EK·oh), a sound wave that has bounced back to its source, as to the person who caused the sound wave to be sent out, 21

egg, a reproductive cell produced by a female organism. When sperm from a male unites with it, the egg is fertilized and can grow into a new organism, 184

element (EL·ih·ment), a substance made up of only one kind of atom, 108

ellipse (ih·LIPS), an oval in which both ends are alike, 264

embryo (EM·bree·oh), a young living animal as it forms inside an egg, or a young living plant inside a seed, 198

energy, the ability to do work; that is, to make matter move, 38

environment (en·VY·ron·ment), all the things and conditions around the place where a plant or animal lives, 137

evaporate (ih·VAP·uh·rayt), to change from a liquid to a gas, 64. Heat energy makes molecules of a liquid move farther apart. In **evaporation,** molecules of the liquid escape and mix with the air.

expand (ik·SPAND), to move farther apart and take up more space. In **expansion,** molecules move farther apart, 71

fat, a compound of carbon, hydrogen, and oxygen; fat molecules have a higher proportion of carbon and hydrogen atoms, and fewer oxygen atoms, than do starch and sugar molecules, 149

fertilizer (FUR·til·i·zer), a substance added to the soil to replace compounds taken from the soil by growing plants, 144

fish ladder, a series of small falls and pools that help salmon go up a river, past high dams built by man, 183

focus (FOH·kus), to bring to a point, as to focus light, 40

food chain, a series of organisms, usually starting with a green plant, in which each organism is used as food by the next one in the series, 180

force, a push or pull. A force may make something move, 226

friction, a force at the surface of an object that makes it hard to move another object across it. Friction causes heat when objects are rubbed together, 272

full moon, the round shape of the Moon when its entire lighted face is seen, 258

fungi (FUN·jy), *singular* **fungus** (FUN·gus) plants, such as bread mold or yeast, that have no chlorophyll and therefore cannot make their own food, 158

gas, any substance that spreads out to fill the container it is placed in. Molecules are far apart and each molecule can move freely, 17

gill (gil), a structure in a fish that enables it to take in oxygen dissolved in water, 192

glacier (GLAY·shur), a moving river of ice, 83

gravitation (grav·ih·TAY·sh'n), the pull every object has on every other object; for example, the pull of the Earth and Moon upon each other, 265

habitat (HAB·ih·tat), the special environment of a living thing, 189

half moon, the Moon at the time that

only one half of its lighted face is seen, 258

humus (HYOO·mus), bits of decayed plants and animals in soil, 161

hypothesis (hy·POTH·eh·sis), an explanation of an event, which is meant to be tested by investigation, 115

inborn, within a living thing at birth. Some behavior may be inborn, 204

lens, a piece of glass shaped in a special way to bend rays of light, 40

liquid (LIK·wid), any substance that pours and changes shape to fit the part of the container into which it is poured. Molecules in a liquid can move easily, 17

matter, anything that has weight and takes up space

membrane, thin skin around an egg or a cell, 198

meteor (MEE·tee·or), a piece of rock from space that glows as it becomes heated from friction when it passes through the layer of air around the Earth, 270

meteorite (MEE·tee·uh·ryt), a piece of rock from space that reaches the Earth before completely burning up in the atmosphere, 273

microscope (MY·kra·skohp), a tool which magnifies objects and makes them seem much larger than they are

migration (my·GRAY·sh'n), the traveling back and forth of certain living things. Wild ducks migrate south in the fall, and come north again in the spring, 201

model (MOD·l), something designed or built to help a person understand or explain an object or event, 50

molecule (MOL·eh·kyool), smallest part there can be of any substance without its being changed, 15

mouth, the place where a river meets the sea, 238

new moon, the Moon when its dark side is facing Earth, 258

nitrate (NY·trayt), a compound of nitrogen and oxygen needed by green plants for good growth, 142

orbit (OR·bit), the path of one object around another in space, as that of the Moon around the Earth, 258

oxygen cycle, the series of changes in which oxygen is taken in and carbon dioxide given off by animals, and the carbon dioxide is used by green plants and oxygen given off by them, 126

phosphate (FOS·fayt), a compound of phosphorus and oxygen needed by green plants for good growth, 142

pitch, highness or lowness of a sound, 8

polarized plastic (POH·luh·riz'd PLAS·tik), plastic that allows only light waves vibrating in a particular direction to pass through, 50

pressure (PRESH·shur), a steady push against each part of a surface, 111

protein (PROH·tee·in), a compound of carbon, hydrogen, oxygen, and nitrogen, and often of sulfur and phosphorus, 149

protozoan (proh·teh·ZOH·en), a tiny single-celled animal, 179

reflected, bounced off an object, as light off a mirror, 32

reservoir (REZ·ir·vwahr), a lake, usually artificial, in which a city's water supply is collected and stored, 90

response, an answer (reaction) a living thing makes to a change in its environment, 207

retina (RET·ih·nuh), the inner, back part of the eye that senses light, 41

root hairs, small hairlike structures on the roots of plants. Water and dissolved substances enter the plant through its root hairs, 86

sediment (SED·ih·ment), bits of rock, soil, leaves, and other substances that settle out from water carrying them, 236

solid (SOL·lid), any substance that has a fixed shape. Molecules in a solid are close together and move very little, 17

sound wave, movement of molecules back and forth in air or other matter in response to vibrations in an object, 16

spawn (spaun), to lay eggs (refers to fish), 184

sperm, a reproductive cell produced by the male. When sperm unites with an egg, the egg can grow into a new organism, 184

spore, a living cell of certain plants that is capable of dividing and developing into a new plant; fungi and ferns produce spores, 159

stimulus (STIM·yoo·lus), anything that makes a living thing react in some way, 207

theory (THEE·uh·ree), a scientist's explanation of objects and events observed; an explanation of the facts, which stands up under testing, 17

vibration (vy·BRAY·sh'n), a regular back and forth movement of matter in any direction; a plucked rubber band vibrates, 6

volcano (vol·KAH·noh), an opening in the Earth's crust from which melted rock inside the Earth flows; also, the mountain formed by this action, 246

water cycle, the changing of molecules of water from liquid to vapor and back to liquid again, 93

watershed, the area from which streams and rivers collect water from rain and melted snow, 88

water table, the level to which water rises in the ground, 91

water vapor, water in the form of an invisible gas, 64

wave, pattern of vibrations that come one after another, 12

INDEX

iron oxide (rust), 105, 107, 109, 115, 116, 119

jack-in-the-pulpit, 138, **139**
Japan Current (Kuroshio), **82,** 83, 84
juncos, migration of, 206–07
Jupiter, 276, **276**

Kuroshio (Japan Current), **82,** 83, 84

Labrador Current, 83
land, building up, 234–38, **236, 237,** 245, **245,** 248; *see also* soil
learned behavior, 208, **208,** 209
leaves, as cover for soil, 241, 242, **242**
lens: investigation into light through, 39, **39;** light bent by, 39, **39,** 40, **40;** light focused by, 39, **39,** 40, **40,** 41, **41;** *see also* convex lens
life cycle: of eel, 205; of mallard duck, **199,** 199–201, **201,** 202, 209; of protozoan, **294,** 294–95, **295;** of salmon, 186, 194, **194,** 196, 202, 209, 216, **216,** 294, **294**
light, 30, **30,** 43, 45, **45,** 52; absorbed, 32, **32,** 35; bent, 38–42, **39, 40, 41, 42;** concept of, 55, 58, 59; diffused, 33, **33,** 34; focused, 39, **39,** 40, **40,** 41, **41;** investigations into, 31, **31,** 39, **39,** 47, **47,** 49, **49;** and molecules in chemical change, 44, 46, 47, **47,** 48; as particles or waves, 51; polarized, 49, **49,** 50, 51; reflected, 32, **32,** 33, **33,** 34, 35; sound compared with, **35,** 35–37, **36;** speed of, 48; straight-line travel of, 36, **6;** travel of, through space, 36, 37; as waves or particles, 51
limewater, as test for carbon dioxide, 46, 47, **47,** 120
liquid, 17, **17,** 131; water as, 17
lungs, 165

magnifying glass, 39, **39**
mallard ducks, 197, **197,** 199, **199;** adapted to environment, 207, 208, 209; at breeding grounds, 200, 201; eggs of, 197, 199; life cycle of, **199,** 199–201, **201,** 202, 209; migration of, **200,** 201, 205, 206, 207, 208; nests of, 197, **197,** 200, 201, 205; young, 199, **199,** 200, 201
man, adapted to environment, 165–66
maple tree, 138, **138**
matter: kinds of, 131; made of atoms and molecules, 131
medicine dropper, 110, **110,** 111–12, 289, **289**
membrane, in egg, 198, **198,** 199
meteorite, 273, **273**
meteors, 270, 272, **272,** 273; investigation into, 271, **271;** showers of, 274
microscope, **289,** 289–90; bacteria seen through, 162, **162;** cells seen through, 154, **154,** 155, **155;** hairs seen through, 290, **290,** 291, **291;** life in drop of water seen through, 292–93, **293,** 300; paper seen through, 33, **33;** use of, **290,** 290–91, **291,** 292–94, **293**
migration, **200,** 201, 205, 206–07, 208. 209
mirror, light reflected from, 30, 32, **32,** 33, 34
Mississippi River, mouth of, 238, **238**
model(s): of behavior of polarized light, 50, **50,** 51, **51;** made by scientists, 50; of molecule of glucose, 148, **149;** of molecule of sucrose, 148, **148;** of molecule of water, 64, **64;** of orbit of comet, 263, **263;** of river, 200, 221, **221,** 234, **234,** 236; of water-purifying plant, 89, **89;** of well, 91, **91**
molds, 158, 158, **159,** 161, 251–52
molecular theory, 17; use of, 17–18, 24

molecules, 15, 17, 62; of air, 15, **15**, 16, 22, 25, 71, 103 (table), 127; atoms in, 131, 132; of carbon dioxide, 108, **108**, 127, 133, **133**; in chemical change, 44, 46, 47, **47**, 48, 133; of copper, 108; in gas, 18; of glucose, 148, **149**; investigation of, in rusting, 113, **113**; in liquid, 18; matter made of, 131; motion of, 25–26, 36, 69; motion of, increased by heat energy, 69, 70, 71, 94; necessary for sound to travel, 36–37; of nitrogen, 108; of oxygen, 107, 108, 131, 132, 133; in solid, 17, 22; of sucrose, 148, **148**; of water, 62, 64, **64**, 65, 93, 94, **108**, 131, **131**, 132, 133

Moon: changing shapes of, 256, **256**, 258, 259; no air on, 37; orbit of, 258, **258**, 259, 266, 277; photographs of far side of, 259, **259**; pulled by Earth's gravitation, 266, **266**

mosses, 157, **157**, 161

moth, inborn behavior of, 205, 207

mountains: breaking down, 224, **224**, 227, **227**, 280; rising, **245**, 245–48, **246**, **247**, 249, 281

mouse, Priestley's experiments with, 123, 124

mouth of river, 238, **238**

mushrooms, 145

Neptune, 269, 277

nest-building, 205, **205**

new moon, 258

Newton, Isaac, 262, 264, 265, 268

nitrates, 142, 144

nitrogen, 103 (table), 108

oak, white, *see* white oak

orbit: of comet, 261, 262, 263, **263**, 264; of Earth, 277, 281; of Moon, 258, **258**, 259, 266, 277

oriole, nest of, 205, **205**

oxygen, 103; in air, 103, 116, 119, 123, 127; atoms of, 107, **107**, 108; and breathing, 123, 128, 133; and burning, 123, 128; in carbon dioxide, 108, **108**, 121, 122, 133, **133**; as element, 108, 127; and gills of fish, 192, 215; given off by green plants, 124, 126, **126**, 128, **128**; in hydrogen peroxide, 103, 104, 109, 119; investigation into air and, 104, **104**, 105, **105**, 106, **106**; iron combined with, 105, 106, 109, **113**, 115, **115**, 117, 119; molecules of, 107, 108, 131, 132, 133; in rocks, 119; in soil, 119; in sugar, 108, **109**, 148; taken in by animals, 128, **128**; uses of, 119, 127; in water, 108, **108**, 119, 132, 133

oxygen cycle, 126, **126**, 128, **128**

Pacific Ocean, life in, 181, **181**

paraffin, 43, 44, 45, **45**, 46

paramecium, **179**, **293**, **295**

parr, 186, 194

phosphates, 142, 144

physical change, 133

pitch of sound, 8; changing, 10–11; investigation into, 9, **9**, 10, **10**; and vibrations, 9, **9**, 10, **10**, 25

plants: ancient, disappearance of, 281; cells of, 154, **154**, 155, **155**, 158; green, *see* green plants; investigation into *Elodea*, 125, **125**; investigation into force exerted by growing, 232, **232**; rocks broken down by, 230, **230**; water in, 85, 86; *see also* tree(s)

polarized plastic, 49, **49**, 50, 51

pond life, 168, **169**, 178, **178**, 179, **179**, 285, 286, **286**, 287, **287**, **292**, 292–95, **293**, **294**, **295**

potato, 149

predictions, by scientists, 274, 275, 276, 277, 282–83

pressure, *see* air pressure

Priestley, Joseph, 123

protein, 149

protozoans, 179, **179**, 217; growing of, 287–88, **288**, 289; life cycle of, **294**, 294–95, **295**

rain, 76, 78–79, 80, 88, 93, 224, 227, 230, 243

reflected light, 32, **32**, 33, **33**, 34, 35

refrigerator, 96, 97

reproduction in living things, 214, **214**, 216; by fission, **294**, 295, 298

reservoir, 90

response to stimulus, 207

retina, 41, **41**

rhubarb, 149

river: model of, 220, 221, **221**, 234, **234**, 236; mouth of, 238, **238**; soil carried by, 220, **220**, 222, **222**, 236, **236**, 237, **237**, 245

robins: migration of, 205; nests of, 205, **205**

rock: breaking down, 224, **224**, 227, **227**, 228, 229, **229**, 230, **230**, 237, 280, **280**; contraction and expansion of, **229**, 280, **280**

rock layer, water held by, 91, **91**, 92

rocket, 259

Rocky Mountains, **218**, 219

root hairs, 86, **86**

roots, soil held by, 240, **241**

root tip cells, 155

rust (iron oxide), 105, 107, 109, 115, 116, 119

salmon, 180, 181, 182, **182**, 186, 189; adapted to environment, 189, 191, **191**, 196, 207, 208, 209, 299; eggs of, 176, **176**, 179, 180, 182, 184, **184**, 185, **185**, 186, 193, 194, 196, 216; hatching of, 185, **185**, 194, 196, 200; journey to ocean, 186, 206; journey to river where hatched, 182–85, **183**, 193; life cycle of, 186, 194, **194**, 196, 202, 209, 216, **216**, 294, **294**; at spawning ground, **184**, 184–85, 193, **193**; sperm of, 184, 193; young, 176, **176**, 179, 180, 184, 185, **185**, 186, **186**, 194, 196, 216, 217

sandstone, 119, **119**

scale, used for weighing, **87**

scales of fish, 191

sediment, 236, 237, 238, 245, 246, 247, 249

seedlings, 164, **164**, 165, 166, 167, 170, 215

seeds, 136, **136**, 137, 150, 230; investigation into force of sprouting, 231, **231**

settling tank, in water purifying plant, 90, **90**

shad, 205

shadow, 31, **31**

silicon, 119

slide, 289, **289**, 290, **290**, 291, **291**, 292

smolt, 186, **186**, 194

snail, **160**, 161; eggs of, 186, 187, **187**

snow, 79, 88, 93

soil: carried by running water, 220, **220**, 222, **222**, 227, **227**, 234, 236, **236**, 237, **237**, 240, 245; cover for, 240–41, 242, **242**, 243; enriched by decayed wood, 170; fertilizers for, 144; holding, 240–43, **241**, **242**; substances in, 142, **142**, 144, 146; substances in, investigation into, 143, **143**; and Van Helmont's investigation, 140, **140**, 141; *see also* land

solid, 17, **17**, 22, 131; water as, 17

water carriers, 88, **88**
water cycle, 93, **93**, 94, **94**
watershed, 90
water table, 91
water vapor, 64, 65, 66, 68, 74, 75, 76, 78, 93, 94; cloud made from condensed, 75; condensation of, 68, 70, 75, 76, 78, 93; *see also* water, as gas
waves, 12, **12**; investigation into, 13, **13**; light, 51; sound, *see* sound waves
web, spider's, **204**, 205
well, 91, 92
wheat plant, 144, **144**
white oak, 157, 158, 163; environment of, 167, 217; seedling of, 164, **164**, 166, 167, 215
wild ducks, *see* mallard ducks
willow tree: environment of, 166–67; Van Helmont's investigation into, **140**, 140–41, **141**, 144, 145
windmill, 91, **91**
wood, decaying, 161, **161**, 170
work, and energy, 46

yeast, 103, 104, 105, 107, 109, 171–72
yolk, egg, 178, 198, 199
yolk sac, of young salmon, **176**, **185**, 194, 200

Zion National Park, 21, **21**

C   0
D   1
E   2
F   3
G   4
H   5
I   6
J   7
    8